Casenote Legal Briefs™

TAXATION

Adaptable to courses utilizing Burke and Friel's casebook on Taxation of Individual Income

NORMAN S. GOLDENBERG, SENIOR EDITOR
PETER TENEN, MANAGING EDITOR

STAFF WRITERS

DAVID KNOBLOCK
HOWARD SCOTT LEVIANT

PUBLISHED BY CASENOTES PUBLISHING CO., INC. 1640 5th ST., SUITE 208 SANTA MONICA, CA 90401

ISBN 0-87457-252-5

FORMAT OF THE CASENOTE LEGAL BRIEF

CASE CAPSULE: This bold-faced section (first three paragraphs) highlights the procedural nature of the case, a short summary of the facts, and the rule of law. This is an invaluable quick-review device designed to refresh the student's memory for classroom discussion and exam preparation.

NATURE OF CASE: This section identifies the form of action (e.g., breach of contract, negligence, battery), the type of proceeding (e.g., demurrer, appeal from trial court's jury instructions) and the relief sought (e.g., damages, injunction, criminal sanctions).

FACT SUMMARY: The fact summary is included to refresh the student's memory. It can be used as a quick reminder of the facts when the student is chosen by an instructor to brief a case.

CONCISE RULE OF LAW: This portion of the brief summarizes the general principle of law that the case illustrates. Like the fact summary, it is included to refresh the student's memory. It may be used for instant recall of the court's holding and for classroom discussion or home review.

FACTS: This section contains all relevant facts of the case, including the contentions of the parties and the lower court holdings. It is written in a logical order to give the student a clear understanding of the case. The plaintiff and defendant are identified by their proper names throughout and are always labeled with a (P) or (D).

ISSUE: The issue is a concise question that brings out the essence of the opinion as it relates to the section of the casebook in which the case appears. Both substantive and procedural issues are included if relevant to the decision.

HOLDING AND DECISION: This section offers a clear and in-depth discussion of the rule of the case and the court's rationale. It is written in easy-to-understand language. When relevant, it includes a thorough discussion of the exceptions listed by the court, the concurring and dissenting opinions, and the names of the judges.

CONCURRENCE / DISSENT: All concurrences and dissents are briefed whenever they are included by the casebook editor.

EDITOR'S ANALYSIS: This last paragraph gives the student a broad understanding of where the case "fits in" with other cases in the section of the book and with the entire course. It is a hornbook-style discussion indicating whether the case is a majority or minority opinion and comparing the principal case with other cases in the casebook. It may also provide analysis from restatements, uniform codes, and law review articles. The editor's analysis will prove to be invaluable to classroom discussion.

CROSS-REFERENCE TO OUTLINE: Wherever possible, following each case is a cross-reference linking the subject matter of the issue to the appropriate place in the *Casenote Law Outline,* which provides further information on the subject.

WINTER v. G.P. PUTNAM'S SONS

938 F.2d 1033 (1991).

NATURE OF CASE: Appeal from summary judgment in a products liability action.

FACT SUMMARY: Winter (P) relied on a book on mushrooms published by Putnam (D) and became critically ill after eating a poisonous mushroom.

CONCISE RULE OF LAW: Strict products liability is not applicable to the expressions contained within a book.

FACTS: Winter (P) purchased The Encyclopedia of Mushrooms, a book published by Putnam (D), to help in collecting and eating wild mushrooms. In 1988, Winter (P), relying on descriptions in the book, ate some wild mushrooms which turned out to be poisonous. Winter (P) became so ill he required a liver transplant. He brought a strict products liability action against Putnam (D), alleging that the book contained erroneous and misleading information that caused his injury. Putnam (D) responded that the information in the book was not a product for purposes of strict products liability, and the trial court granted its motion for summary judgment. The trial court also rejected Winter's (P) actions for negligence and misrepresentation. Winter (P) appealed.

ISSUE: Is strict products liability applicable to the expressions contained within a book?

HOLDING AND DECISION: (Sneed, J.) No. Strict products liability is not applicable to the expressions contained within a book. Products liability is geared toward tangible objects. The expression of ideas is governed by copyright, libel, and misrepresentation laws. The Restatement (Second) of Torts lists examples of the items that are covered by §402A strict liability. All are tangible items, such as tires or automobiles. There is no indication that the doctrine should be expanded beyond this area. Furthermore, there is a strong public interest in the unfettered exchange of ideas. The threat of liability without fault could seriously inhibit persons who wish to share thoughts and ideas with others. Although some courts have held that aeronautical charts are products for purposes of strict liability, these charts are highly technical tools which resemble compasses. The Encyclopedia of Mushrooms, published by Putnam (D), is a book of pure thought and expression and therefore does not constitute a product for purposes of strict liability. Additionally, publishers do not owe a duty to investigate the contents of books that they distribute. Therefore, a negligence action may not be maintained by Winter (P) against Putnam (D). Affirmed.

EDITOR'S ANALYSIS: This decision is in accord with the rulings in most jurisdictions. See Alm v. Nostrand Reinhold Co., Inc., 480 N.E. 2d 1263 (Ill. 1985). The court also stated that since the publisher is not a guarantor of the accuracy of an author's statements, an action for negligent misrepresentation could not be maintained. The elements of negligent misrepresentation are stated in § 311 of the Restatement (Second) of Torts.

[For more information on misrepresentation, see Casenote Law Outline on Torts, Chapter 12, § III, Negligent Misrepresentation.]

NOTE TO THE STUDENT

OUR GOAL. It is the goal of Casenotes Publishing Company, Inc. to create and distribute the finest, clearest and most accurate legal briefs available. To this end, we are constantly seeking new ideas, comments and constructive criticism. As a user of *Casenote Legal Briefs,* your suggestions will be highly valued. With all correspondence, please include your complete name, address, and telephone number, including area code and zip code.

THE TOTAL STUDY SYSTEM. Casenote Legal Briefs are just one part of the Casenotes TOTAL STUDY SYSTEM. Most briefs are (wherever possible) cross-referenced to the appropriate *Casenote Law Outline,* which will elaborate on the issue at hand. By purchasing a Law Outline together with your Legal Brief, you will have both parts of the Casenotes TOTAL STUDY SYSTEM. (See the advertising in the front of this book for a list of Law Outlines currently available.)

A NOTE ABOUT LANGUAGE. Please note that the language used in *Casenote Legal Briefs* in reference to minority groups and women reflects terminology used within the historical context of the time in which the respective courts wrote the opinions. We at Casenotes Publishing Co., Inc. are well aware of and very sensitive to the desires of all people to be treated with dignity and to be referred to as they prefer. Because such preferences change from time to time, and because the language of the courts reflects the time period in which opinions were written, our case briefs will not necessarily reflect contemporary references. We appreciate your understanding and invite your comments.

A NOTE REGARDING NEW EDITIONS. As of our press date, this Casenote Legal Brief is current and includes briefs of all cases in the current version of the casebook, divided into chapters that correspond to that edition of the casebook. However, occasionally a new edition of the casebook comes out in the interim, and sometimes the casebook author will make changes in the sequence of the cases in the chapters, add or delete cases, or change the chapter titles. Should you be using this Legal Brief in conjuction with a casebook that was issued later than this book, you can receive all of the newer cases, which are available free from us, by sending in the "Supplement Request Form" in this section of the book (please follow all instructions on that form). The Supplement(s) will contain all the missing cases, and will bring your Casenote Legal Brief up to date.

EDITOR'S NOTE. Casenote Legal Briefs are intended to supplement the student's casebook, not replace it. There is no substitute for the student's own mastery of this important learning and study technique. If used properly, *Casenote Legal Briefs* are an effective law study aid that will serve to reinforce the student's understanding of the cases.

REV 4-97

REF. # 1219-97-497

SUPPLEMENT REQUEST FORM

At the time this book was printed, a brief was included for every major case in the casebook and for every existing supplement to the casebook. However, if a new supplement to the casebook (or a new edition of the casebook) has been published since this publication was printed and if that casebook supplement (or new edition of the casebook) was available for sale at the time you purchased this Casenote Legal Briefs book, we will be pleased to provide you the new cases contained therein AT NO CHARGE when you send us a stamped, self-addressed envelope.

TO OBTAIN YOUR FREE SUPPLEMENT MATERIAL, **YOU MUST FOLLOW THE INSTRUCTIONS BELOW PRECISELY** OR YOUR REQUEST WILL NOT BE ACKNOWLEDGED!

1. Please check if there is in fact an existing supplement and, if so, that the cases are not already included in your Casenote Legal Briefs. Check the main table of cases as well as the supplement table of cases, if any.
2. **REMOVE THIS ENTIRE PAGE FROM THE BOOK.** You MUST send this ORIGINAL page to receive your supplement. This page acts as your proof of purchase and contains the reference number necessary to fill your supplement request properly. No photocopy of this page or written request will be honored or answered. Any request from which the reference number has been removed, altered or obliterated will not be honored.

✶ 3. Prepare a STAMPED self-addressed envelope for return mailing. Be sure to use a FULL SIZE (9 X 12) ENVELOPE (MANILA TYPE) so that the supplement will fit and AFFIX ENOUGH POSTAGE TO COVER 3 OZ. **ANY SUPPLEMENT REQUEST NOT ACCOMPANIED BY A STAMPED SELF-ADDRESSED ENVELOPE WILL ABSOLUTELY NOT BE FILLED OR ACKNOWLEDGED.**

4. MULTIPLE SUPPLEMENT REQUESTS: If you are ordering more than one supplement, we suggest that you enclose a stamped, self-addressed envelope for each supplement requested. If you enclose only one envelope for a multiple request, your order may not be filled immediately should any supplement which you requested still be in production. In other words, your order will be held by us until it can be filled completely.
5. Casenotes prints two kinds of supplements. A "New Edition" supplement is issued when a new edition of your casebook is published. A "New Edition" supplement gives you all major cases found in the new edition of the casebook which did not appear in the previous edition. A regular "supplement" is issued when a paperback supplement to your casebook is published. If the box at the lower right is stamped, then the "New Edition" supplement was provided to your bookstore and is *not* available from Casenotes; however, Casenotes will still send you any regular "supplements" which have been printed either before or after the new edition of your casebook appeared and which, according to the reference number at the top of this page, have not been included in this book. If the box is not stamped, Casenotes will send you any supplements, "New Edition" and/or regular, needed to completely update your Casenote Legal Briefs.

✶☞ ***NOTE:*****REQUESTS FOR SUPPLEMENTS WILL NOT BE FILLED UNLESS THESE INSTRUCTIONS ARE COMPLIED WITH!**

6. Fill in the following information:

Full title of CASEBOOK **TAXATION**

CASEBOOK author's name **Burke and Friel**

Copyright year of new edition or new paperback supplement ___

Name and location of bookstore where this Casenote Legal Brief was purchased ___

Name and location of law school you attend ___

Any comments regarding Casenote Legal Briefs ___

NOTE: IF THIS BOX IS STAMPED, NO NEW EDITION SUPPLEMENT CAN BE OBTAINED BY MAIL.

PUBLISHED BY CASENOTES PUBLISHING CO., INC. 1640 5th ST, SUITE 208 SANTA MONICA, CA 90401

PLEASE PRINT

NAME ___ **PHONE** ___ **DATE** ___

ADDRESS/CITY/STATE/ZIP ___

Announcing the First *Totally Integrated* Law Study System

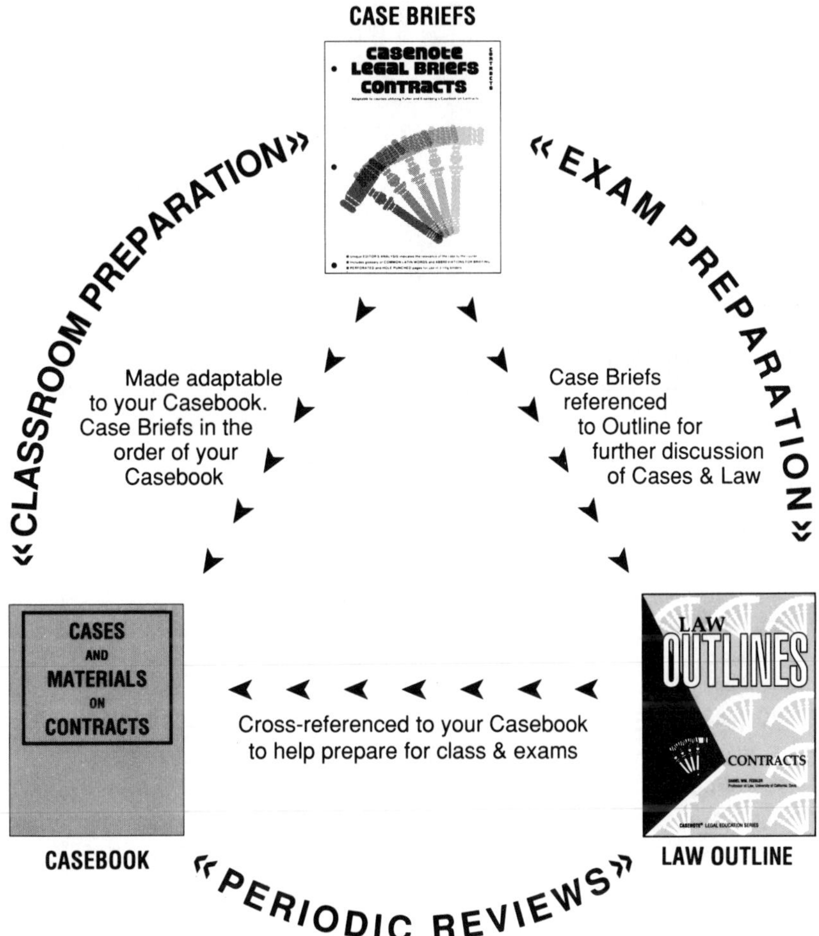

Casenotes Integrated Study System Makes Studying Easier and More Effective Than Ever!

Casenotes has just made studying easier and more effective than ever before, because we've done the work for you! Through our exclusive integrated study system, most briefs found in this volume of Casenote Legal Briefs are cross-referenced to the corresponding area of law in the Casenote Law Outline series. The cross-reference immediately follows the Editor's Analysis at the end of the brief, and it will direct you to the corresponding chapter and section number in the Casenote Law Outline for further information on the case or the area of law.

This cross-referencing feature will enable you to make the most effective use of your time. While each Casenote Law Outline focuses on a particular subject area of the law, each legal briefs volume is adapted to a specific casebook. Now, with cross-referencing of Casenote Legal Briefs to Casenote Law Outlines, you can have the best of both worlds – briefs for all major cases in your casebooks and easy-to-find, easy-to-read explanations of the law in our Law Outline series. Casenote Law Outlines are authored exclusively by law professors who are nationally recognized authorities in their field. So using Casenote Law Outlines is like studying with the top law professors.

Try Casenotes new totally integrated study system and see just how easy and effective studying can be.

Casenotes Integrated Study System Does The Work For You!

casenote™ LEGAL BRIEFS

PRICE LIST — EFFECTIVE JULY 1, 1997 • PRICES SUBJECT TO CHANGE WITHOUT NOTICE

Ref. No.	Course	Adaptable to Courses Utilizing	Retail Price
1265	ADMINISTRATIVE LAW	BONFIELD & ASIMOV	17.00
1263	ADMINISTRATIVE LAW	BREYER, STEWART & SUNSTEIN	19.00
1266	ADMINISTRATIVE LAW	CASS, DIVER & BEERMAN	17.00
1260	ADMINISTRATIVE LAW	GELLHORN, B., S., R., S. & F.	17.00
1264	ADMINISTRATIVE LAW	MASHAW, MERRILL & SHANE	18.50
1267	ADMINISTRATIVE LAW	REESE	17.00
1262	ADMINISTRATIVE LAW	SCHWARTZ	18.00
1290	ADMIRALTY	HEALY & SHARPE	21.00
1350	AGENCY & PARTNERSHIP (ENT.ORG)	CONARD, KNAUSS & SIEGEL	21.00
1351	AGENCY & PARTNERSHIP	HYNES	20.00
1281	ANTITRUST (TRADE REGULATION)	HANDLER, P., G., & W.	17.50
1283	ANTITRUST	SULLIVAN & HOVENKAMP	18.00
1611	BANKING LAW	MACEY & MILLER	17.00
1303	BANKRUPTCY (DEBTOR-CREDITOR)	EISENBERG	19.00
1040	CIVIL PROCEDURE	COUND, F., M. & S	20.00
1043	CIVIL PROCEDURE	FIELD, KAPLAN & CLERMONT	20.00
1041	CIVIL PROCEDURE	HAZARD, TAIT & FLETCHER	19.00
1047	CIVIL PROCEDURE	MARCUS, REDISH & SHERMAN	19.00
1044	CIVIL PROCEDURE	ROSENBERG, S. & D.	20.00
1046	CIVIL PROCEDURE	YEAZELL	17.00
1311	COMM'L LAW	FARNSWORTH, H., R., H. & M.	19.00
1312	COMM'L LAW	JORDAN & WARREN	19.00
1310	COMM'L LAW (SALES/SEC.TR./PAY.LAW [Sys.])	SPEIDEL, SUMMERS & WHITE	22.00
1313	COMM'L LAW (SALES/SEC.TR./PAY.LAW)	WHALEY	19.00
1320	COMMUNITY PROPERTY	BIRD	17.50
1630	COMPARATIVE LAW	SCHLESINGER, B., D., & H.	16.00
1048	COMPLEX LITIGATION	MARCUS & SHERMAN	17.00
1072	CONFLICTS	BRILMAYER	17.00
1071	CONFLICTS	CRAMTON, C. K., & K.	17.00
1070	CONFLICTS	ROSENBERG, HAY & W.	20.00
1086	CONSTITUTIONAL LAW	BREST & LEVINSON	18.00
1082	CONSTITUTIONAL LAW	COHEN & VARAT	21.00
1088	CONSTITUTIONAL LAW	FARBER, ESKRIDGE & FRICKEY	18.00
1080	CONSTITUTIONAL LAW	GUNTHER & SULLIVAN	20.00
1081	CONSTITUTIONAL LAW	LOCKHART, K., C., S. & F.	18.00
1085	CONSTITUTIONAL LAW	ROTUNDA	20.00
1087	CONSTITUTIONAL LAW	STONE, S., S. & T.	19.00
1102	CONTRACTS	BURTON	20.00
1017	CONTRACTS	CALAMARI, PERILLO & BENDER	23.00
1101	CONTRACTS	CRANDALL & WHALEY	20.00
1014	CONTRACTS	DAWSON, HARVEY & H.	19.00
1010	CONTRACTS	FARNSWORTH & YOUNG	18.00
1011	CONTRACTS	FULLER & EISENBERG	20.00
1100	CONTRACTS	HAMILTON, RAU & WEINTRAUB	19.00
1013	CONTRACTS	KESSLER, GILMORE & KRONMAN	23.00
1016	CONTRACTS	KNAPP & CRYSTAL	20.50
1012	CONTRACTS	MURPHY & SPEIDEL	22.00
1018	CONTRACTS	MURRAY	22.00
1015	CONTRACTS	ROSETT	21.00
1019	CONTRACTS	VERNON	20.00
1502	COPYRIGHT	GOLDSTEIN	18.00
1501	COPYRIGHT	NIMMER, M., M., & N.	19.50
1218	CORPORATE TAXATION	LIND, S. L. & R	14.00
1050	CORPORATIONS	CARY & EISENBERG	19.00
1054	CORPORATIONS	CHOPER,COFFEE, & GILSON	21.50
1350	CORPORATIONS (ENTERPRISE ORG.)	CONARD, KNAUSS & SIEGEL	21.00
1053	CORPORATIONS	HAMILTON	19.00
1057	CORPORATIONS	O'KELLEY & THOMPSON	18.00
1056	CORPORATIONS	SOLOMON, S., B., & W.	19.00
1052	CORPORATIONS	VAGTS	17.00
1300	CREDITOR'S RIGHTS (DEBTOR-CREDITOR)	RIESENFELD	21.00
1550	CRIMINAL JUSTICE	WEINREB	18.00
1029	CRIMINAL LAW	BONNIE, C., J., & L.	17.00
1020	CRIMINAL LAW	BOYCE & PERKINS	22.00
1028	CRIMINAL LAW	DRESSLER	21.00
1027	CRIMINAL LAW	JOHNSON	20.00
1021	CRIMINAL LAW	KADISH & SCHULHOFER	19.00
1026	CRIMINAL LAW	KAPLAN, WEISBERG & BINDER	18.00
1023	CRIMINAL LAW	LAFAVE	19.00
1205	CRIMINAL PROCEDURE	ALLEN, KUHNS & STUNTZ	17.00
1202	CRIMINAL PROCEDURE	HADDAD, Z., S. & B.	20.00
1200	CRIMINAL PROCEDURE	KAMISAR, LAFAVE & ISRAEL	19.00
1204	CRIMINAL PROCEDURE	SALTZBURG & CAPRA	17.00
1203	CRIMINAL PROCEDURE (PROCESS)	WEINREB	18.50
1303	DEBTOR-CREDITOR	EISENBERG	19.00
1300	DEBTOR-CREDITOR (CRED. RTS.)	RIESENFELD	21.00
1304	DEBTOR-CREDITOR	WARREN & WESTBROOK	19.00
1224	DECEDENTS ESTATES	RITCHIE, ALFORD, EFFLAND & D.	21.00
1222	DECEDENTS ESTATES	SCOLES & HALBACH	21.50
1231	DECEDENTS ESTATES (TRUSTS)	WAGGONER, A. & F.	20.00
	DOMESTIC RELATIONS (*see* FAMILY LAW)		
3000	EDUCATION LAW (COURSE OUTLINE)	AQUILA & PETZKE	25.50
1670	EMPLOYMENT DISCRIMINATION	FRIEDMAN & STRICKLER	17.00
1671	EMPLOYMENT DISCRIMINATION	ZIMMER, SULLIVAN, R. & C.	18.00
1660	EMPLOYMENT LAW	ROTHSTEIN, KNAPP & LIEBMAN	19.50
1350	ENTERPRISE ORGANIZATION	CONARD, KNAUSS & SIEGEL	21.00
1342	ENVIRONMENTAL LAW	ANDERSON, MANDELKER & T.	16.00
1341	ENVIRONMENTAL LAW	FINDLEY & FARBER	18.00
1345	ENVIRONMENTAL LAW	MENELL & STEWART	17.00
1344	ENVIRONMENTAL LAW	PERCIVAL, MILLER, S. & L.	18.00
1343	ENVIRONMENTAL LAW	PLATER, ABRAMS & GOLDFARB	17.00
	EQUITY (*see* REMEDIES)		
1217	ESTATE & GIFT TAXATION	BITTKER, CLARK & McCOUCH	15.00
	ETHICS (*see* PROFESSIONAL RESPONSIBILITY)		
1065	EVIDENCE	GREEN & NESSON	20.00
1066	EVIDENCE	MUELLER & KIRKPATRICK	17.00
1064	EVIDENCE	STRONG, BROUN & M..	22.50
1062	EVIDENCE	SUTTON & WELLBORN	22.00
1061	EVIDENCE	WALTZ & PARK	20.00
1060	EVIDENCE	WEINSTEIN, M., A. & B.	22.50
1244	FAMILY LAW (DOMESTIC RELATIONS)	AREEN	22.00
1242	FAMILY LAW (DOMESTIC RELATIONS)	CLARK & GLOWINSKY	19.00
1245	FAMILY LAW (DOMESTIC RELATIONS)	ELLMAN, KURTZ & BARTLETT	20.00
1243	FAMILY LAW (DOMESTIC RELATIONS)	KRAUSE	24.00
1240	FAMILY LAW (DOMESTIC RELATIONS)	WADLINGTON	20.00
1231	FAMILY PROPERTY LAW (WILLS/TRUSTS)	WAGGONER, A. & F.	20.00
1362	FEDERAL COURTS	CURRIE	17.00
1360	FEDERAL COURTS	FALLON, M. & S. (HART & W.)	19.00
1360	FEDERAL COURTS	HART & WECHSLER (FALLON)	19.00
1363	FEDERAL COURTS	LOW & JEFFRIES	16.00
1361	FEDERAL COURTS	McCORMICK, C. & W.	20.00
1364	FEDERAL COURTS	REDISH & NICHOL	17.00
1510	GRATUITOUS TRANSFERS	CLARK, LUSKY & MURPHY	18.00
1650	HEALTH LAW	FURROW, J., J., & S.	17.50
1640	IMMIGRATION LAW	ALEINIKOFF, MARTIN & M.	16.00
1641	IMMIGRATION LAW	LEGOMSKY	18.00
1371	INSURANCE LAW	KEETON	21.00
1372	INSURANCE LAW	YORK, WHELAN & MARTINEZ	19.00
1370	INSURANCE LAW	YOUNG & HOLMES	17.00
1394	INTERNATIONAL BUSINESS TRANSACTIONS	FOLSOM, GORDON & SPANOGLE	15.00
1393	INTERNATIONAL LAW	CARTER & TRIMBLE	16.00
1392	INTERNATIONAL LAW	HENKIN, P., S. & S.	17.00
1390	INTERNATIONAL LAW	OLIVER, F., B., S., & W.	22.00
1331	LABOR LAW	COX, BOK, GORMAN & FINKIN	19.00
1332	LABOR LAW	HARPER & ESTREICHER	20.00
1333	LABOR LAW	LESLIE	18.50
1330	LABOR LAW	MERRIFIELD, S. & C.	19.00
1471	LAND FINANCE (REAL ESTATE TRANS)	BERGER & JOHNSTONE	18.00
1620	LAND FINANCE (REAL ESTATE TRANS)	NELSON & WHITMAN	19.00
1452	LAND USE	CALLIES, FREILICH & ROBERTS	17.00
1450	LAND USE	WRIGHT & GITELMAN	23.00
1421	LEGISLATION	ESKRIDGE & FRICKEY	15.00
1480	MASS MEDIA	FRANKLIN & ANDERSON	15.00
1312	NEGOTIABLE INSTRUMENTS (COMM. LAW)	JORDAN & WARREN	19.00
1313	NEGOTIABLE INSTRUMENTS (COMM. LAW)	WHALEY	18.00
1541	OIL & GAS	KUNTZ, L., A. & S.	18.00
1540	OIL & GAS	MAXWELL, WILLIAMS, M. & K.	18.00
1560	PATENT LAW	FRANCIS & COLLINS	23.00
1310	PAYMENT LAW [SYST.][COMM. LAW]	SPEIDEL, SUMMERS & WHITE	22.00
1313	PAYMENT LAW (COMM.LAW / NEG. INST.)	WHALEY	19.00
1431	PRODUCTS LIABILITY	OWEN, MONTGOMERY & K.	20.00
1091	PROF. RESPONSIBILITY (ETHICS)	GILLERS	13.00
1093	PROF. RESPONSIBILITY (ETHICS)	HAZARD, KONIAK, & CRAMTON	18.00
1092	PROF. RESPONSIBILITY (ETHICS)	MORGAN & ROTUNDA	13.00
1030	PROPERTY	CASNER & LEACH	21.00
1031	PROPERTY	CRIBBET, J., F. & S.	21.50
1037	PROPERTY	DONAHUE, KAUPER & MARTIN	18.00
1035	PROPERTY	DUKEMINIER & KRIER	18.00
1034	PROPERTY	HAAR & LIEBMAN	20.50
1036	PROPERTY	KURTZ & HOVENKAMP	19.00
1033	PROPERTY	NELSON, STOEBUCK, & W.	20.50
1032	PROPERTY	RABIN & KWALL	20.00
1038	PROPERTY	SINGER	18.50
1621	REAL ESTATE TRANSACTIONS	GOLDSTEIN & KORNGOLD	18.00
1471	REAL ESTATE TRANS. & FIN. (LAND FINANCE)	BERGER & JOHNSTONE	18.00
1620	REAL ESTATE TRANSFER & FINANCE	NELSON & WHITMAN	18.00
1254	REMEDIES (EQUITY)	LAYCOCK	20.00
1253	REMEDIES (EQUITY)	LEAVELL, L., N. & K/F.	21.00
1252	REMEDIES (EQUITY)	RE & RE	23.00
1255	REMEDIES (EQUITY)	SHOBEN & TABB	22.50
1250	REMEDIES (EQUITY)	YORK, BAUMAN & RENDLEMAN	25.00
1312	SALES (COMM. LAW)	JORDAN & WARREN	19.00
1310	SALES (COMM. LAW)	SPEIDEL, SUMMERS & WHITE	22.00
1313	SALES (COMM. LAW)	WHALEY	19.00
1312	SECURED TRANS. (COMM. LAW)	JORDAN & WARREN	19.00
1310	SECURED TRANS.	SPEIDEL, SUMMERS & WHITE	22.00
1313	SECURED TRANS. (COMM. LAW)	WHALEY	19.00
1272	SECURITIES REGULATION	COX, HILLMAN, LANGEVOORT	18.00
1270	SECURITIES REGULATION	JENNINGS, MARSH & COFFEE	18.00
1680	SPORTS LAW	WEILER & ROBERTS	17.50
1217	TAXATION (ESTATE & GIFT)	BITTKER, CLARK & McCOUCH	15.00
1219	TAXATION (INDIV. INC.)	BURKE & FRIEL	19.00
1212	TAXATION (FED. INC.)	FREELAND, LIND & STEPHENS	18.00
1211	TAXATION (FED. INC.)	GRAETZ & SCHENK	17.00
1210	TAXATION (FED. INC.)	KLEIN & BANKMAN	18.00
1218	TAXATION (CORPORATE)	LIND, S., L. & R.	14.00
1006	TORTS	DOBBS	19.00
1003	TORTS	EPSTEIN	20.50
1004	TORTS	FRANKLIN & RABIN	17.50
1001	TORTS	HENDERSON, P. & S.	20.50
1000	TORTS	PROSSER, W., S., K., & P.	24.00
1005	TORTS	SHULMAN, JAMES & GRAY	22.00
1281	TRADE REGULATION (ANTITRUST)	HANDLER, P., G., & W.	17.50
1230	TRUSTS	BOGERT, O., H., & H.	20.50
1231	TRUSTS/WILLS (FAMILY PROPERTY LAW)	WAGGONER, A. & F.	20.00
1410	U.C.C	EPSTEIN, MARTIN, H. & N.	15.00
1223	WILLS, TRUSTS & ESTATES	DUKEMINIER & JOHANSON	19.00
1220	WILLS	MECHEM & ATKINSON	20.00
1231	WILLS/TRUSTS (FAMILY PROPERTY LAW)	WAGGONER, A. & F.	20.00

(SERIES XI.)

CASENOTES PUBLISHING CO. INC. ● 1640 FIFTH STREET, SUITE 208 ● SANTA MONICA, CA 90401 ● (310) 395-6500

E-Mail Address- casenote@westworld.com

Website-http://www.casenotes.com

PLEASE PURCHASE FROM YOUR LOCAL BOOKSTORE. IF UNAVAILABLE, YOU MAY ORDER DIRECT.*

4TH CLASS POSTAGE (ALLOW TWO WEEKS) $1.00 PER ORDER; 1ST CLASS POSTAGE $3.00 (ONE BOOK), $2.00 EACH (TWO OR MORE BOOKS)

*CALIF. RESIDENTS PLEASE ADD 8¼% SALES TAX

NOTES

A GLOSSARY OF COMMON LATIN WORDS AND PHRASES ENCOUNTERED IN THE LAW

A FORTIORI: Because one fact exists or has been proven, therefore a second fact that is related to the first fact must also exist.

A PRIORI: From the cause to the effect. A term of logic used to denote that when one generally accepted truth is shown to be a cause, another particular effect must necessarily follow.

AB INITIO: From the beginning; a condition which has existed throughout, as in a marriage which was void ab initio.

ACTUS REUS: The wrongful act; in criminal law, such action sufficient to trigger criminal liability.

AD VALOREM: According to value; an ad valorem tax is imposed upon an item located within the taxing jurisdiction calculated by the value of such item.

AMICUS CURIAE: Friend of the court. Its most common usage takes the form of an amicus curiae brief, filed by a person who is not a party to an action but is nonetheless allowed to offer an argument supporting his legal interests.

ARGUENDO: In arguing. A statement, possibly hypothetical, made for the purpose of argument, is one made arguendo.

BILL QUIA TIMET: A bill to quiet title (establish ownership) to real property.

BONA FIDE: True, honest, or genuine. May refer to a person's legal position based on good faith or lacking notice of fraud (such as a bona fide purchaser for value) or to the authenticity of a particular document (such as a bona fide last will and testament).

CAUSA MORTIS: With approaching death in mind. A gift causa mortis is a gift given by a party who feels certain that death is imminent.

CAVEAT EMPTOR: Let the buyer beware. This maxim is reflected in the rule of law that a buyer purchases at his own risk because it is his responsibility to examine, judge, test, and otherwise inspect what he is buying.

CERTIORARI: A writ of review. Petitions for review of a case by the United States Supreme Court are most often done by means of a writ of certiorari.

CONTRA: On the other hand. Opposite. Contrary to.

CORAM NOBIS: Before us; writs of error directed to the court that originally rendered the judgment.

CORAM VOBIS: Before you; writs of error directed by an appellate court to a lower court to correct a factual error.

CORPUS DELICTI: The body of the crime; the requisite elements of a crime amounting to objective proof that a crime has been committed.

CUM TESTAMENTO ANNEXO, ADMINISTRATOR (ADMINISTRATOR C.T.A.): With will annexed; an administrator c.t.a. settles an estate pursuant to a will in which he is not appointed.

DE BONIS NON, ADMINISTRATOR (ADMINISTRATOR D.B.N.): Of goods not administered; an administrator d.b.n. settles a partially settled estate.

DE FACTO: In fact; in reality; actually. Existing in fact but not officially approved or engendered.

DE JURE: By right; lawful. Describes a condition that is legitimate "as a matter of law," in contrast to the term "de facto," which connotes something existing in fact but not legally sanctioned or authorized. For example, de facto segregation refers to segregation brought about by housing patterns, etc., whereas de jure segregation refers to segregation created by law.

DE MINIMUS: Of minimal importance; insignificant; a trifle; not worth bothering about.

DE NOVO: Anew; a second time; afresh. A trial de novo is a new trial held at the appellate level as if the case originated there and the trial at a lower level had not taken place.

DICTA: Generally used as an abbreviated form of obiter dicta, a term describing those portions of a judicial opinion incidental or not necessary to resolution of the specific question before the court. Such nonessential statements and remarks are not considered to be binding precedent.

DUCES TECUM: Refers to a particular type of writ or subpoena requesting a party or organization to produce certain documents in their possession.

EN BANC: Full bench. Where a court sits with all justices present rather than the usual quorum.

EX PARTE: For one side or one party only. An ex parte proceeding is one undertaken for the benefit of only one party, without notice to, or an appearance by, an adverse party.

EX POST FACTO: After the fact. An ex post facto law is a law that retroactively changes the consequences of a prior act.

EX REL.: Abbreviated form of the term ex relatione, meaning, upon relation or information. When the state brings an action in which it has no interest against an individual at the instigation of one who has a private interest in the matter.

FORUM NON CONVENIENS: Inconvenient forum. Although a court may have jurisdiction over the case, the action should be tried in a more conveniently located court, one to which parties and witnesses may more easily travel, for example.

GUARDIAN AD LITEM: A guardian of an infant as to litigation, appointed to represent the infant and pursue his/her rights.

HABEAS CORPUS: You have the body. The modern writ of habeas corpus is a writ directing that a person (body) being detained (such as a prisoner) be brought before the court so that the legality of his detention can be judicially ascertained.

IN CAMERA: In private, in chambers. When a hearing is held before a judge in his chambers or when all spectators are excluded from the courtroom.

IN FORMA PAUPERIS: In the manner of a pauper. A party who proceeds in forma pauperis because of his poverty is one who is allowed to bring suit without liability for costs.

INFRA: Below, under. A word referring the reader to a later part of a book. (The opposite of supra.)

IN LOCO PARENTIS: In the place of a parent.

IN PARI DELICTO: Equally wrong; a court of equity will not grant requested relief to an applicant who is in pari delicto, or as much at fault in the transactions giving rise to the controversy as is the opponent of the applicant.

IN PARI MATERIA: On like subject matter or upon the same matter. Statutes relating to the same person or things are said to be in pari materia. It is a general rule of statutory construction that such statutes should be construed together, i.e., looked at as if they together constituted one law.

IN PERSONAM: Against the person. Jurisdiction over the person of an individual.

IN RE: In the matter of. Used to designate a proceeding involving an estate or other property.

IN REM: A term that signifies an action against the res, or thing. An action in rem is basically one that is taken directly against property, as distinguished from an action in personam, i.e., against the person.

INTER ALIA: Among other things. Used to show that the whole of a statement, pleading, list, statute, etc., has not been set forth in its entirety.

INTER PARTES: Between the parties. May refer to contracts, conveyances or other transactions having legal significance.

INTER VIVOS: Between the living. An inter vivos gift is a gift made by a living grantor, as distinguished from bequests contained in a will, which pass upon the death of the testator.

IPSO FACTO: By the mere fact itself.

JUS: Law or the entire body of law.

LEX LOCI: The law of the place; the notion that the rights of parties to a legal proceeding are governed by the law of the place where those rights arose.

MALUM IN SE: Evil or wrong in and of itself; inherently wrong. This term describes an act that is wrong by its very nature, as opposed to one which would not be wrong but for the fact that there is a specific legal prohibition against it (malum prohibitum).

MALUM PROHIBITUM: Wrong because prohibited, but not inherently evil. Used to describe something that is wrong because it is expressly forbidden by law but that is not in and of itself evil, e.g., speeding.

MANDAMUS: We command. A writ directing an official to take a certain action.

MENS REA: A guilty mind; a criminal intent. A term used to signify the mental state that accompanies a crime or other prohibited act. Some crimes require only a general mens rea (general intent to do the prohibited act), but others, like assault with intent to murder, require the existence of a specific mens rea.

MODUS OPERANDI: Method of operating; generally refers to the manner or style of a criminal in committing crimes, admissible in appropriate cases as evidence of the identity of a defendant.

NEXUS: A connection to.

NISI PRIUS: A court of first impression. A nisi prius court is one where issues of fact are tried before a judge or jury.

N.O.V. (NON OBSTANTE VEREDICTO): Notwithstanding the verdict. A judgment n.o.v. is a judgment given in favor of one party despite the fact that a verdict was returned in favor of the other party, the justification being that the verdict either had no reasonable support in fact or was contrary to law.

NUNC PRO TUNC: Now for then. This phrase refers to actions that may be taken and will then have full retroactive effect.

PENDENTE LITE: Pending the suit; pending litigation underway.

PER CAPITA: By head; beneficiaries of an estate, if they take in equal shares, take per capita.

PER CURIAM: By the court; signifies an opinion ostensibly written "by the whole court" and with no identified author.

PER SE: By itself, in itself; inherently.

PER STIRPES: By representation. Used primarily in the law of wills to describe the method of distribution where a person, generally because of death, is unable to take that which is left to him by the will of another, and therefore his heirs divide such property between them rather than take under the will individually.

PRIMA FACIE: On its face, at first sight. A prima facie case is one that is sufficient on its face, meaning that the evidence supporting it is adequate to establish the case until contradicted or overcome by other evidence.

PRO TANTO: For so much; as far as it goes. Often used in eminent domain cases when a property owner receives partial payment for his land without prejudice to his right to bring suit for the full amount he claims his land to be worth.

QUANTUM MERUIT: As much as he deserves. Refers to recovery based on the doctrine of unjust enrichment in those cases in which a party has rendered valuable services or furnished materials that were accepted and enjoyed by another under circumstances that would reasonably notify the recipient that the rendering party expected to be paid. In essence, the law implies a contract to pay the reasonable value of the services or materials furnished.

QUASI: Almost like; as if; nearly. This term is essentially used to signify that one subject or thing is almost analogous to another but that material differences between them do exist. For example, a quasi-criminal proceeding is one that is not strictly criminal but shares enough of the same characteristics to require some of the same safeguards (e.g., procedural due process must be followed in a parol hearing).

QUID PRO QUO: Something for something. In contract law, the consideration, something of value, passed between the parties to render the contract binding.

RES GESTAE: Things done; in evidence law, this principle justifies the admission of a statement that would otherwise be hearsay when it is made so closely to the event in question as to be said to be a part of it, or with such spontaneity as not to have the possibility of falsehood.

RES IPSA LOQUITUR: The thing speaks for itself. This doctrine gives rise to a rebuttable presumption of negligence when the instrumentality causing the injury was within the exclusive control of the defendant, and the injury was one that does not normally occur unless a person has been negligent.

RES JUDICATA: A matter adjudged. Doctrine which provides that once a court of competent jurisdiction has rendered a final judgment or decree on the merits, that judgment or decree is conclusive upon the parties to the case and prevents them from engaging in any other litigation on the points and issues determined therein.

RESPONDEAT SUPERIOR: Let the master reply. This doctrine holds the master liable for the wrongful acts of his servant (or the principal for his agent) in those cases in which the servant (or agent) was acting within the scope of his authority at the time of the injury.

STARE DECISIS: To stand by or adhere to that which has been decided. The common law doctrine of stare decisis attempts to give security and certainty to the law by following the policy that once a principle of law as applicable to a certain set of facts has been set forth in a decision, it forms a precedent which will subsequently be followed, even though a different decision might be made were it the first time the question had arisen. Of course, stare decisis is not an inviolable principle and is departed from in instances where there is good cause (e.g., considerations of public policy led the Supreme Court to disregard prior decisions sanctioning segregation).

SUPRA: Above. A word referring a reader to an earlier part of a book.

ULTRA VIRES: Beyond the power. This phrase is most commonly used to refer to actions taken by a corporation that are beyond the power or legal authority of the corporation.

ADDENDUM OF FRENCH DERIVATIVES

IN PAIS: Not pursuant to legal proceedings.

CHATTEL: Tangible personal property.

CY PRES: Doctrine permitting courts to apply trust funds to purposes not expressed in the trust but necessary to carry out the settlor's intent.

PER AUTRE VIE: For another's life; in property law, an estate may be granted that will terminate upon the death of someone other than the grantee.

PROFIT A PRENDRE: A license to remove minerals or other produce from land.

VOIR DIRE: Process of questioning jurors as to their predispositions about the case or parties to a proceeding in order to identify those jurors displaying bias or prejudice.

Notes

TABLE OF CASES

Continued on next page

Notes

TABLE OF CASES (Continued)

CHAPTER 2*
GROSS INCOME: CONCEPTS AND LIMITATIONS

QUICK REFERENCE RULES OF LAW

1. **Realization, Imputed Income and Bargain Purchases.** Money received as punitive damages must be included as gross income. (Commissioner v. Glenshaw Glass Co.)

   [For more information on sources of gross income, see Casenote Law Outline on Federal Income Taxation, Chapter 3, § II, No Source Requirement]

2. **Realization, Imputed Income and Bargain Purchases.** Unless expressly excluded by law, gross income includes all income from whatever source derived. (Cesarini v. United States)

   [For more information on the definition of gross income, see Casenote Law Outline on Federal Income Taxation, Chapter 3, § II, No Source Requirement.]

3. **Realization, Imputed Income and Bargain Purchases.** The payment by an employer of the income taxes assessed against his employee constitute additional taxable income to the employee. (Old Colony Trust Co. v. Commissioner)

   [For more information on discharged debt as gross income, see Casenote Law Outline on Federal Income Taxation, Chapter 3, § III, Realized Increase in Net Wealth (or Net Worth).]

4. **Realization, Imputed Income and Bargain Purchases.** When services are paid for in a form other than money, the fair market value of the thing received must be included in gross income. (McCann v. United States)

   [For more information on nonmonetary receipts as gross income, see Casenote Law Outline on Federal Income Taxation, Chapter 3, § I, No Requirement That Income Must Take the Form of Cash.]

5. **Realization, Imputed Income and Bargain Purchases.** The purchase of property for less than its fair market value does not, of itself, give rise to the realization of taxable income. (Pellar v. Commissioner)

   [For more information on deferred realization of gross income, see Casenote Law Outline on Federal Income Taxation, Chapter 3, § IV, Some Instances in Which Gross Income (Other Than Gain) Is Deferred Pending Some Later "Realization" Event.]

***There are no cases in Chapter 1.**

Notes

COMMISSIONER v. GLENSHAW GLASS CO.

348 U.S. 426 (1955).

NATURE OF CASE: Appeal by the Commissioner (D) of a Tax Court ruling in favor of a taxpayer.

FACT SUMMARY: Glenshaw (P) settled a lawsuit for $800,000, a portion of which it sought to exclude from gross income as punitive damages for fraud.

CONCISE RULE OF LAW: Money received as punitive damages must be included as gross income.

FACTS: Glenshaw Glass (P) was involved in protracted litigation with Hartford-Empire Company. Glenshaw (P) sought exemplary damages for fraud and treble damages due to antitrust violations. The suit was settled, and Glenshaw (P) received roughly $800,000. A method of allocation determined that $324,529.94 represented payment for punitive damages for fraud and antitrust violations. Glenshaw (P) did not report this amount on its taxes. The Commissioner (D) noticed a deficiency and Glenshaw (P) filed suit in Tax Court on the matter, where it prevailed. On appeal, the court of appeals upheld the decision for the taxpayer. The Commissioner (D) appealed to the Supreme Court.

ISSUE: Must money received as punitive damages recovery be reported as gross income?

HOLDING AND DECISION: (Warren, C.J.) Yes. Money received as punitive damages must be included as gross income. The definition of gross income, promulgated by Congress, begins from an all-inclusive standpoint. Receipts are assumed to be gross income unless an exclusion removes them from the category. In this case, Glenshaw (P) has an undeniable accession to wealth. The fact that the payments were extracted from wrongdoers as punishment for unlawful conduct does not detract from the characterization as gross income. Reversed.

EDITOR'S ANALYSIS: This case provides a simple example of how courts analyze gross income. The very broad statutory definition is given full effect and deference. Essentially, a rough starting point is that everything is gross income unless explicitly excluded.

[For more information on sources of gross income, see Casenote Law Outline on Federal Income Taxation, Chapter 3, § II, No Source Requirement.]

NOTES:

CESARINI v. UNITED STATES

296 F. Supp. 3 (N.D. Ohio 1969).

NATURE OF CASE: Action by taxpayers for recovery of income tax payments.

FACT SUMMARY: The Cesarinis (P), after finding money in a piano and declaring it on their taxes, filed an amended tax return which removed the funds in question from gross income.

CONCISE RULE OF LAW: Unless expressly excluded by law, gross income includes all income from whatever source derived.

FACTS: In 1957, Mr. and Mrs. Cesarini (P) purchased a used piano. In 1964, while cleaning the piano, they discovered $4,467 in old currency. The original owner of the money was unascertainable, and the Cesarinis (P) exchanged the old currency for new. They then declared the money as ordinary income from other sources on their 1964 joint income tax return. On October 18, 1965, the Cesarinis (P) filed an amended return eliminating the sum of $4,467 from the gross income computation and requesting a refund in the amount of $836.51, the tax paid on the discovered funds. On January 18, 1966, the Commissioner of Internal Revenue (D) rejected the refund claim in its entirety. The Cesarinis (P) filed an action in U.S. District Court to recover the taxes paid on the discovered funds.

ISSUE: Is money found by chance excludable from gross income since the tax code does not contain a section expressly taxing treasure trove?

HOLDING AND DECISION: (Young, J.) No. Unless expressly excluded by law, gross income includes all income from whatever source derived. Section 61(a) of Title 26 U.S.C. is the starting point for determining what should be included in gross income. The definition of gross income is expansive, limited only by express exclusion of specific items. The Supreme Court has frequently held that such all-inclusive language defining gross income was intended by Congress to reach the full measure of its taxing power under the Sixteenth Amendment. In this case, the Cesarinis (P) increased their wealth by the discovery of treasure trove. They argue that since Congress recently enacted code sections that expressly included the value of prizes and awards in gross income computation, and specifically exempted gifts, the intent was to place treasure trove in the category of gift, making treasure trove nontaxable. But this argument overlooks the basic principle that unless an explicit exemption can be identified, income from any source is included in gross income calculation. The Cesarinis' (P) claim is denied.

EDITOR'S ANALYSIS: Finding a comprehensive definition of income has proven nearly impossible. The solution has generally been to start with the proposition that any benefit received is income, and then remove specific circumstances from the definition. In this case, discovered wealth is not exempted from the definition of gross income, thus becoming taxable. And since there isn't a compelling reason, such as misplaced economic incentives, to exempt treasure trove, it is unlikely to ever be exempted from the definition.

[For more information on the definition of gross income, see Casenote Law Outline on Federal Income Taxation, Chapter 3, § II, No Source Requirement.]

NOTES:

OLD COLONY TRUST CO. v. COMMISSIONER

279 U.S. 716 (1929).

NATURE OF CASE: Appeal from a finding of tax deficiency.

FACT SUMMARY: The Commissioner (P) sought to tax, as additional income to the employee, the amount of his federal income taxes which were paid on his behalf by his employer.

CONCISE RULE OF LAW: The payment by an employer of the income taxes assessed against his employee constitute additional taxable income to the employee.

FACTS: The American Woolen Company's board of directors resolved that the company should pay the federal income taxes assessed upon the incomes of certain of its officers including its president, Wood. Wood's taxes for the years 1918 and 1919 totaled slightly more than $1,000,000, and were paid by the company. The Commissioner (P) argued that that payment amounted to additional income to Wood and was taxable as income to him. The Board of Tax Appeals upheld the Commissioner's (P) position, and this appeal followed. (The status of Old Colony (D) was not explained in the case excerpt.)

ISSUE: Does the payment by an employer of the income taxes assessed against his employee constitute additional taxable income to the employee?

HOLDING AND DECISION: (Taft, C.J.) Yes. The payment by an employer of the income taxes assessed against his employee constitutes additional taxable income to the employee. The payment of the tax by the employer was in consideration of the services rendered by the employee and was a gain derived by the employee from his labor. The form of payment is irrelevant. The discharge by a third person of an obligation to him is equivalent to receipt by the person taxed. Further, the taxes were paid upon a valuable consideration, namely, the services rendered by the employee and as part of the consideration for such services. Nor was the payment of taxes a gift. Even though the payment was entirely voluntary, it was nevertheless compensation. Affirmed.

EDITOR'S ANALYSIS: The same result was reached in the following cases: (1) United States v. Boston and Main-R., 279 U.S. 732 (1929), where the lessee railroad paid the taxes on its lessor's income; (2) Ethel S. Amey, 22 T.C. 756 (1954), where a lease provided that the lessee, in addition to paying rent directly to the lessor, should make mortgage payments on the property; and (3) Sachs v. Commissioner, 277 F.2d 879 (8th Cir. 1960), where a corporation paid fines levied on its president. In Rev. Rule, 68-507, 1968-z C.B. 485, IRS held that payments made to a minister by his church in order to help him to pay his self-employment tax were taxable income to him.

[For more information on discharged debt as gross income, see Casenote Law Outline on Federal Income Taxation, Chapter 3, § III, Realized Increase in Net Wealth (or Net Worth).]

NOTES:

McCANN v. UNITED STATES

81-2 T.C. 9689 (1981), 696 F.2d 1386 (Fed.Cir. 1983).

NATURE OF CASE: Review of judgment denying claim for refund.

FACT SUMMARY: The McCanns (P) received an all-expense-paid trip as a reward for Mrs. McCann's job performance, but they did not include the value of the trip in their gross income calculation on their joint income tax returns.

CONCISE RULE OF LAW: When services are paid for in a form other than money, the fair market value of the thing received must be included in gross income.

FACTS: Mrs. McCann (P) was employed by Security Industrial Insurance Company. In 1973, she was awarded an all-expense-paid trip to Las Vegas, based upon her exceptional job performance for Security. Only 47 of 400 Security employees met the target sales goals to qualify for the trip. While the trip was referred to as a sales seminar, the trip was almost entirely for leisure. Roughly two hours of the three-day trip were substantively related to any aspect of work. The remaining time was spent sight-seeing, attending shows and banquets, and independently enjoying resort activities. The McCanns (P) did not include the value of the trip on their joint tax return for 1973. They were subsequently audited and found to be deficient in the amount of $199.16, plus accrued interest of $64.97. The deficiency was calculated based upon the tax on the cost of the trip to Security. The McCanns (P) paid the amount and then filed a claim for refund. The claim was denied. They then took their claim before the U.S. Claims Court where the court ruled against them, and finally the case was appealed to the U.S. Court of Appeals.

ISSUE: When services are paid for in a form other than money, must the fair market value of the thing received be included in gross income?

HOLDING AND DECISION: (White, J.) Yes. When services are paid for in a form other than money, the fair market value of the thing received must be included in gross income. It is already settled that income need not be in the form of money to be included in gross income for tax purposes. When a company rewards an employee for exceptional performance by providing an all-expense-paid vacation, then clearly the employee has received some benefit. The only difficulty in such a circumstance is determining the value of the noncash payment to the employee. Certainly, different employees would value a trip differently. But since a subjective valuation would be impossible to determine, the cost of supplying the trip stands adequately for the value of the trip. In this case, Security spent over $68,000 on the trip for employees. The taxes on the McCanns' (P) portion was calculated to be $199.16. The McCanns (P) never disputed this method of calculation at trial. Since the trip was effectively a bonus payment, and the value was not disputed, the Claims Court is affirmed.

EDITOR'S ANALYSIS: The issues in this case point toward characterization and valuation. The court took great pains to point out how many of the shows the employees attended were "topless" shows. If the trip were required for business, then the value of the trip would not be included in gross income. And absent any stipulated value for the noncash payment, courts will usually rely upon the actual monetary cost of providing the payment to the employees.

[For more information on nonmonetary receipts as gross income, see Casenote Law Outline on Federal Income Taxation, Chapter 3, § I, No Requirement That Income Must Take the Form of Cash.]

NOTES:

PELLAR v. COMMISSIONER
25 T.C. 299 (1955), acq.

NATURE OF CASE: Suit contesting IRS calculation of gross income.

FACT SUMMARY: The Pellars (P) paid $55,000 for a house fairly valued at $70,000, but paid no taxes on the $15,000 difference which they realized.

CONCISE RULE OF LAW: The purchase of property for less than its fair market value does not, of itself, give rise to the realization of taxable income.

FACTS: The Pellars (P) entered into an agreement with a construction company for the building of a dwelling. The price was fixed in advance at $40,000. After adding extras for the Pellars (P) and correcting construction errors, the actual cost of construction was substantially higher than the set price. However, the contractor was content to take a small loss on the job since Sam Briskin, father of Rosalie Pellar (P), was involved with several corporations that had employed the contractor for well over one million dollars in work. The contractor stuck with the arranged price in the hopes of keeping and extending the goodwill of Sam Briskin. The completed house was valued on the market at $70,000. The Pellars (P) spent $15,000 on preparing the land for construction. Added to the $40,000 construction costs, the Pellars (P) spent only $55,000 on the house. The IRS (D) assessed the Pellars (P) with a deficiency in taxes on the $15,000 not included in their gross income. The Pellars (P) then sought to have the deficiency notice overturned in Tax Court.

ISSUE: Does the purchase of property for less than its fair market value give rise to the realization of taxable income?

HOLDING AND DECISION: (Fisher, J.) No. The purchase of property for less than its fair market value does not, of itself, give rise to the realization of taxable income. A realization of income normally arises and is taxed upon sale or other disposition of a piece of property. Thus, if a property is purchased for less than market value and then sold later at market value, the difference will be taxed as profit, and the property owner has not avoided taxation on the extra profit. The only exception arises if the purchase price is so unreasonably low as to indicate a sham exchange or the inclusion of other consideration. In this case, however, there are no clear facts to suggest that the Pellars (P) realized any income. While the contractor did hope to maintain goodwill with Sam Briskin, there was no guarantee of future work or referrals. The contractor merely made the business decision to accept a small loss for potential future business. The Pellars (P) will be responsible for taxes on the extra potential profits at any time in the future that they choose to sell the property. Decision entered for the Pellars (P).

EDITOR'S ANALYSIS: Part of what underlies the general rule in this case is the need to determine when to apply a tax on realized profits on real property. Allowing the buyer to defer any tax burden until the time of sale appeals to common sense. Given the generally high cost of real property, the buyer would be dissuaded from purchasing if a tax payment had to be made in full at the time of purchase. Money received at the time of sale reduces the burden of paying tax on the realized profit.

[For more information on deferred realization of gross income, see Casenote Law Outline on Federal Income Taxation, Chapter 3, § IV, Some Instances in Which Gross Income (Other Than Gain) Is Deferred Pending Some Later "Realization" Event.]

NOTES:

Notes

CHAPTER 3
THE EFFECT OF AN OBLIGATION TO REPAY

QUICK REFERENCE RULES OF LAW

1. **The Effect of an Obligation to Repay.** No income has been earned where a company might never receive it and has no right to demand payment. (North American Oil Consolidated v. Burnet)

   [For more information on accounting methods, see Casenote Law Outline on Federal Income Taxation, Chapter 8, § II, Tax Accounting Methods.]

2. **The Effect of an Obligation to Repay.** All unlawful gains, including embezzled funds, are to be included in gross income in the year in which the funds or other property are misappropriated. (James v. United States)

   [For more information on illegal gains and income, see Casenote Law Outline on Federal Income Taxation, Chapter 3, § II, No Source Requirement.]

3. **The Effect of an Obligation to Repay.** A taxpayer receives income if he acquires earnings without an express or implied obligation to repay and has complete dominion over their disposition. (Commissioner v. Indianapolis Power & Light Company)

   [For more information on security deposits, see Casenote Law Outline on Federal Income Taxation, Chapter 8, § I, The Taxable Year.]

Notes

NORTH AMERICAN OIL CONSOLIDATED v. BURNET

286 U.S. 417 (1932).

NATURE OF CASE: Appeal from assessment of tax liability for income allegedly earned in 1917.

FACT SUMMARY: Income earned in 1916 from property in the hands of a receiver was not reported or given to North American Oil (P) until 1917.

CONCISE RULE OF LAW: No income has been earned where a company might never receive it and has no right to demand payment.

FACTS: North American Oil (P) held oil property owned by the U.S. A suit was begun to oust North American (P), and a receiver was appointed to manage the property and retain the income until the suit was decided. In 1917, the court decided in favor of North American (P) and income earned in 1916 was turned over to it. The government appealed, and the case was finally decided in favor of North American (P) in 1922. The Commissioner determined that the income earned in 1916 should be included in North American's (P) 1917 income and assessed a deficiency tax on this amount. The Board of Tax Appeals found that the income was taxable to the Receiver in 1916, but was overturned by the court of appeals. Certiorari was granted.

ISSUE: Should funds impounded by a Receiver who is in control of only a portion of a corporation's property be taxed to the corporation when it finally has an unqualified right to receive them?

HOLDING AND DECISION: (Brandeis, J.) Yes. First, the income was not taxable to the Receiver in 1916 because he was only in control of a portion of North American's (P) property. This is consistent with long-standing treasury regulations. Next, the income could not be taxed to North American (P) in 1916, because it might never receive the funds. The first time North American (P) had an unqualified right to the funds was after the district court awarded them to it in 1917. At the time the receivership was vacated, North American (P) had a claim for the money and actually received it. The fact that the case was not ultimately settled until 1922 is immaterial. If North American (P) had lost, it would have repaid the funds out of current assets and taken a deduction for that amount. The funds received in 1917 should have been reported as income for that year. The decision of the court of appeals is affirmed.

EDITOR'S ANALYSIS: Other examples of the above-mentioned situation occur where reserves are set up which exceed actual costs or expenditures. And, for the cash or accrual taxpayer, income must be reported when it is received, even if it will not be earned until a subsequent tax year.

[For more information on accounting methods, see Casenote Law Outline on Federal Income Taxation, Chapter 8, § II, Tax Accounting Methods.]

NOTES:

JAMES v. UNITED STATES

366 U.S. 213 (1961).

NATURE OF CASE: Review of court of appeals decision affirming a conviction for tax evasion.

FACT SUMMARY: James (P) embezzled in excess of $738,000 during the years 1951 through 1954, but he did not report these amounts in gross income.

CONCISE RULE OF LAW: All unlawful gains, including embezzled funds, are to be included in gross income in the year in which the funds or other property are misappropriated.

FACTS: James (D) was a union official who embezzled over $738,000 during the years 1951 through 1954 from his employer union and an insurance company. James (D) did not report the embezzled funds on his tax returns as gross income received in those years. He was indicted in federal court and convicted for willfully attempting to evade the federal income tax due in the respective years. James (D) appealed, and the conviction was affirmed by the court of appeals. He then petitioned the Supreme Court for certiorari.

ISSUE: Are embezzled funds to be included in the gross income of the embezzler in the year in which the funds are misappropriated?

HOLDING AND DECISION: (Warren, C.J.) Yes. Expressly overruling Commissioner v. Wilcox, 327 U.S. 404, all unlawful gains, including embezzled funds, are to be included in gross income in the year in which the funds or other property are misappropriated. Congress has extensive powers to levy taxes. Nowhere in the expansive tax code has there been a suggestion that the Congress intended to treat the law-breaking taxpayer any differently from the honest one. At one time, this Court held in Wilcox that embezzled money did not fall into the category of gross income since the embezzler was under an unqualified duty to repay the money to his employer. But the same can be said of any misappropriation. Whether the transfer of legal title occurs or not, the individual has increased his or her wealth. Loans are distinguishable since they must be repaid over a certain period; misappropriated funds might never be detected and recovered. In this case, James (D) gained control over the embezzled funds. Thus, in the applicable years, he should have reported this income on his taxes. However, James' (D) conviction was a felony for willfully failing to account for his taxes or willfully attempting to evade his obligation to pay taxes. Since the Wilcox exception for embezzled funds was in effect at the time of the embezzlement, the element of willfulness could not be proved. Reversed and remanded for dismissal of the indictment.

DISSENT: (Black, J.) The embezzler has the same funds he was entrusted with as an employee. He has gained no title through the embezzlement. By allowing the funds to be subjected to a tax, the United States is taking a preferential claim on money that ought to be restored to the rightful owner. It seems that there is no answer to this argument. It appears that the only result of the holding in this case, which erroneously overrules Wilcox, is to place the federal government in the business of prosecuting embezzlers under the guise of tax evasion.

EDITOR'S ANALYSIS: The problem of a governmental tax claim on embezzled funds would apply to many different types of misappropriation. Any theft of money gives rise to a tax burden on the stolen money, but the rightful owner also has a legal right to seek recovery. Thus the argument for keeping the embezzlement exception in place loses some credibility if all other theft crimes are treated differently.

[For more information on illegal gains and income, see Casenote Law Outline on Federal Income Taxation, Chapter 3, § II, No Source Requirement.]

NOTES:

COMMISSIONER v. INDIANAPOLIS POWER & LIGHT CO.

493 U.S. 203 (1990).

NATURE OF CASE: Appeal from denial of Internal Revenue Service Commissioner deficiency.

FACT SUMMARY: IPL (D) was asserted IRS deficiencies, after it required certain customers to make deposits with it to assure future payment of their electric bills.

CONCISE RULE OF LAW: A taxpayer receives income if he acquires earnings without an express or implied obligation to repay and has complete dominion over their disposition.

FACTS: IPL (D), a public utility, required its electric customers to make deposits to assure prompt payment. The amount of the required deposit was twice the customer's estimated monthly bill. IPL (D) paid interest on the deposits. A customer could get a refund of the deposit by demonstrating acceptable credit. The customer could choose to have the refund applied against subsequent bills. IPL (D) did not treat the deposits as income at the time of receipt. Instead, they were treated as current liabilities. If the deposits were later used to offset a customer's bill, the utility made the necessary accounting adjustments. The IRS Commissioner (P) asserted deficiencies for IPL's (D) accounting practice on the basis that the deposits were advance payments for IPL (D) electricity, and therefore taxable as income in the year of receipt. The Tax Court ruled in favor of IPL (D) on the basis that only 5 percent of IPL (D) customers were required to make deposits; that the customer rather than the utility controlled the ultimate disposition of the deposit; and that IPL (D) consistently treated the payments as loans by the customers by paying the customer's interest on the payments. The court of appeal affirmed the Tax Court's decision. The IRS Commissioner (P) appealed.

ISSUE: Does a taxpayer receive income if he acquires earnings with an express or implied obligation to repay and has no dominion over their disposition?

HOLDING AND DECISION: (Blackmun, J.) No. A taxpayer does not receive income if he acquires earnings without an express or implied obligation to repay and has no dominion over their disposition. IPL (D) asserts that the payments are similar to loans. The IRS Commissioner (P) contends that a deposit to secure payment of future income is analogous to an advance payment over the customer deposits. Rather, these deposits are acquired subject to an express "obligation to repay," either at the time service is terminated or at the time a customer establishes good credit. If the customer makes timely payments his deposit will ultimately be refunded. Both the timing and the method of that refund are largely within the customer's control. It is not dispositive that the deposits are not segregated by the IRS from its other funds. After all, the same might be said of commercial loan proceeds. Even though the deposits frequently will be used to pay for electricity (either because a customer defaults, or a customer chooses to apply the refund of the deposit to future bills), the individual who makes an advance payment retains no right to insist upon return of the funds. So long as the recipient of the payment fulfills the terms of the bargain, he may retain the payment. An IPL customer may insist upon repayment in cash or he may choose to apply the money to the purchase of electricity. Therefore, the utility acquires no unfettered dominion over the money at the time of receipt. Affirmed.

EDITOR'S ANALYSIS: In an analogous case, a state regulatory agency allowed the taxpayer, a public utility, to increase its rates in order to finance the construction of a power plant, subject to the agency's obligation to refund the increase over a thirty-year period after the new plant began operations. The Court rejected the utility's claim that increase amounts should be treated as loans. The Court reasoned that the utility's claim that increase amounts should be treated as loans. The Court reasoned that the utility's obligation to repay was only a declaration of regulatory policy, not a fixed obligation to repay, and that the funds were not segregated to be repaid to the same people from whom they had been collected (Iowa Southern Utilities Co. v. United States, 841 F.2d 1108 (Fed. Cir. 1988)).

[For more information on security deposits, see Casenote Law Outline on Federal Income Taxation, Chapter 8, § I, The Taxable Year.]

NOTES:

Notes

CHAPTER 4
GAINS DERIVED FROM DEALINGS IN PROPERTY

QUICK REFERENCE RULES OF LAW

1. **Basis of Property Acquired in Taxable Exchange.** Where a taxable exchange of property occurs, gain or loss should be recognized in establishing the basis for the property on the date of the transfer. (Philadelphia Park Amusement Co. v. United States.)

   [For more information on the transfer of property, see Casenote Law Outline on Federal Income Taxation, Chapter 4, § II, Amount Realized]

Notes

PHILADELPHIA PARK AMUSEMENT CO. v. UNITED STATES

Cl. Ct., 126 F. Supp. 184 (1954).

NATURE OF CASE: Action to require the allowance of a deduction.

FACT SUMMARY: Philadelphia Park Amusement Co. (P) deeded its interest in a bridge to the city in exchange for a ten-year extension on a franchise.

CONCISE RULE OF LAW: Where a taxable exchange of property occurs, gain or loss should be recognized in establishing the basis for the property on the date of the transfer.

FACTS: Philadelphia Park Amusement Co. (P) obtained a 50-year franchise to operate a railroad service to its amusement park. A bridge was constructed for over $300,000 to operate the railroad. When the franchise was about to expire, Philadelphia Park (P) offered to transfer the bridge to the city in exchange for a ten-year franchise extension. No gain or loss was reported from the transaction. Philadelphia Park (P) later abandoned the railroad service in favor of bus transportation. It (P) then attempted to take a loss deduction from its income based on the abandonment of the franchise. The IRS (D) denied the deduction on the ground that since the bridge had no value and there had been no taxable exchange no loss could be maintained. The Amusement Co. (P) maintained that the value of the franchise was equal to the value of the bridge and it was entitled to take the undepreciated basis as a loss.

ISSUE: Is the basis of property established as of the date of a taxable transfer?

HOLDING AND DECISION: (Laramore, J.) Yes. A transfer of assets, except where exempted by statute, is a taxable event. The taxpayer's basis in the new property is its fair market value as of the date of transfer plus any taxable gain to him associated with the transaction. Where the transfer was made at arms-length and the new asset cannot be valued, it is deemed to be equal to the value of the asset which was given up by the taxpayer. While the franchise extension cannot be valued, we feel the bridge had some value on the date of transfer. This amount should be deemed the basis of the Amusement Co. (P) in the franchise. The undepreciated value of the franchise as of the date of abandonment was a proper deduction. The failure of the Co. (P) to properly record the transaction originally does not prevent it from later establishing the valuations for the purpose of deducting the loss. Reversed and remanded for proper valuation of the bridge and, if possible, the franchise.

EDITOR'S ANALYSIS: The amount paid for an asset is its basis. If the property is later sold for more than its original price, the taxpayer has made a taxable gain. If the taxpayer depreciates the asset over a period of time, his basis is reduced to the extent of the depreciation deductions. If the property is exchange for other than cash, the adjusted basis is the value of the property received, plus any gain which was taxed to the taxpayer as a result of the transaction. If a loss was taken, the adjusted basis is the value of the property received.

[For more information on the transfer of property, see Casenote Law Outline on Federal Income Taxation, Chapter 4, § II, Amount Realized.]

NOTES:

Notes

CHAPTER 5
GIFTS, BEQUESTS AND INHERITANCE

QUICK REFERENCE RULES OF LAW

1. **Part Gift, Part Sale.** The determination as to whether transferred property constitutes a gift requires an analysis by the trier of fact of all relevant factors. (Commissioner v. Duberstein)

   [For more information on gifts, see Casenote Law Outline on Federal Income Taxation, Chapter 3, § V, Exclusions from Gross Income.]

2. **Part Gift, Part Sale.** While gross income will generally not include property acquired by gift, devise, or bequest, where such property is received for the purpose of payment for services performed, it becomes taxable income. (Wolder v. Commissioner)

   [For more information on exclusions from gross income, see Casenote Law Outline on Federal Income Taxation, Chapter 3, § V, Exclusions from Gross Income.]

3. **Part Gift, Part Sale.** Receipts by taxpayers who are engaged in rendering services that are contributed by those with whom the taxpayers have some personal or functional contact are taxable income when in conformity with the practices of the area and easily valued. (Olk v. United States)

Notes

COMMISSIONER v. DUBERSTEIN

363 U.S. 278 (1960).

NATURE OF CASE: Review of reversal of Tax Court decision upholding a determination of a tax deficiency.

FACT SUMMARY: Duberstein (P) was given a car by a business associate but did not declare the car as taxable income, deeming it a gift.

CONCISE RULE OF LAW: The determination as to whether transferred property constitutes a gift requires an analysis by the trier of fact of all relevant factors.

FACTS: Duberstein (P) was the president of Duberstein Iron and Metal Company. For many years the company had done business with Mohawk Metal Corporation, of which Berman was the president. The two presidents did extensive business together, and from time to time, Duberstein (P) would direct potential customers to Berman that were of no interest to Duberstein's (P) company. After receiving particularly useful information, Berman gave Duberstein (P) a Cadillac. Duberstein (P) later testified that he did not believe that he would have been given car had he not provided valuable information. Duberstein (P) did not report the car as gross income, and the Commissioner (D) noticed a deficiency. Duberstein (P) filed suit in Tax Court, but the tax court ruled for the IRS (D). On appeal, the court of appeals reversed. The Commissioner (D) appealed to the Supreme Court.

ISSUE: Does the intent of donor determine whether property consitutes a gift, exempting it from the taxable income of the donee?

HOLDING AND DECISION: (Brennan, J.) No. The determination as to whether transferred property constitutes a gift requires an analysis by the trier of fact of all relevant factors. The meaning of the term "gift," as applied to particular transfers, has always been a matter of contention. The problem is that the statute uses gift in a colloquial sense, rather than a common-law sense. The characterization of the donor is of little use, since the donor would have an incentive to hide business compensation in the guise of gifts. And characterization by the taxpayer is of even lesser value. But were this court to attempt to reconcile all previous decisions on the matter, and promulagate a test to categorize transfers as gifts, it would be painting far too broadly. Thus, each case must be examined on the particular facts, and deference must be given to the findings of the trier of fact. Here, the Tax Court found that the overtone of Berman's gift was a compensation for past services. The transfer was of a sufficiently business-oriented nature to move it outside the gift exclusion. Reversed.

EDITOR'S ANALYSIS: One of the problems with the sweeping language that Congress used as it fashioned the tax code is that courts have less guidance with which to divine the intent of Congress in specific circumstances. Courts have adopted a loose system for dealing with this problem. They expect Congress will enact clarifications or reforms if the courts do not interpret correctly.

[For more information on gifts, see Casenote Law Outline on Federal Income Taxation, Chapter 3, § V, Exclusions from Gross Income.]

NOTES:

WOLDER v. COMMISSIONER

493 F.2d 608 (1974).

NATURE OF CASE: Appeal of Tax Court ruling that stocks and cash received under a will constitute taxable income.

FACT SUMMARY: Wolder (P) agreed to render legal services to a client without billing for them in exchange for money and stocks bequeathed to him in her will.

CONCISE RULE OF LAW: While gross income will generally not include property acquired by gift, devise, or bequest, where such property is received for the purpose of payment for services performed, it becomes taxable income.

FACTS: Wolder (P) and his client, Boyce, entered into a written agreement in 1947. The essence of the agreement was that Wolder (P) would provide Boyce with any legal services she required for the entirety of her life without billing for the services. In exchange, Boyce agreed to bequeath 500 shares of stock to Wolder (P), and any other securities or funds that might come into her possession through her ownership of the original 500 shares. In 1957, Boyce received 750 shares of common stock and 500 shares of convertible preferred in exchange for her original 500 shares as a result of a corporate merger. In 1964, the convertible preferred was redeemed for $15,845. Boyce, true to her agreement, revised her will to bequeath to Wolder (P) the sum of $15,845 and the 750 shares of common stock. Over the course of Boyce's life, Wolder (P) did render legal services to her, though the services consisted largely of revising her will. After he received the legacy, Wolder (P) was found to be deficient in his tax payments for not including it in his gross income. The Tax Court ruled against Wolder (P) in his claim that the bequest was exempt under the tax code, and Wolder (P) appealed to the court of appeals.

ISSUE: Does an individual receive income when he is bequeathed a substantial sum of money in lieu of payment for services rendered?

HOLDING AND DECISION: (Oakes, J.) Yes. While gross income will generally not include property acquired by gift, devise, or bequest, where such property is received for the purpose of payment for services performed, it becomes taxable income. In Commissioner v. Duberstein, 363 U.S. 278 (1960), the Supreme Court held that the true test with respect to gifts was whether the gift was a bona fide gift, or simply a method for paying compensation. Here, there is no dispute that services were rendered to Boyce by Wolder (P). The bequest was, in effect, a delayed payment for the services. Following Boyce's death, the New York Surrogate Court held that Wolder (P) did in fact receive a bequest. But New York law cannot control the Federal power to define what constitutes income. Payment for services falls under the category of gross income, and hiding that payment in the guise of a bequest does not change that fact. Affirmed.

EDITOR'S ANALYSIS: Given the decision in Duberstein, this case is even more clear-cut. In Duberstein, the transfer was made without consideration, with no moral or legal obligation. Here, services were agreed upon and performed, making the bequest very clearly a payment for services rendered.

[For more information on exclusions from gross income, see Casenote Law Outline on Federal Income Taxation, Chapter 3, § V, Exclusions from Gross Income.]

NOTES:

OLK v. UNITED STATES

536 F.2d 876 (9th Cir. 1976).

NATURE OF CASE: Appeal from trial court verdict granting refund of income taxes.

FACT SUMMARY: Olk (P), a craps dealer, claimed that monies known as "tokes" given to him by players at the casino were nontaxable gifts.

CONCISE RULE OF LAW: Receipts by taxpayers who are engaged in rendering services that are contributed by those with whom the taxpayers have some personal or functional contact are taxable income when in conformity with the practices of the area and easily valued.

FACT SUMMARY: Olk (P) was a craps dealer at two Las Vegas casinos. It was common practice for about 5% of the players at these casinos to voluntarily give money to the dealers or to place bets for them. These "tokes" were given to the dealers as a result of impulsive generosity or superstition on the part of players, and not as a form of compensation for services. The tokes given to the dealers were placed in a common pool and equally divided among them at the end of each shift. Olk (P) received between ten and twenty dollars a day as his share of the tokes. He claimed that the tokes qualified as nontaxable gifts. The trial court agreed, and the Commissioner (D) appealed.

ISSUE: Are receipts by taxpayers engaged in rendering services that are contributed by those with whom the taxpayers have some personal or functional contact taxable income?

HOLDING AND DECISION: (Sneed, J.) Yes. Receipts by taxpayers engaged in rendering services that are contributed by those with whom the taxpayers have some personal or functional contact are taxable income when in conformity with the practices of the area and easily valued. Whether a receipt qualifies as a nontaxable gift depends on the basic reason for the donor's conduct, that is, the donor's dominant motive. If the dominant motive is detached and disinterested generosity, then the receipt is considered a nontaxable gift. In this case, however, tokes by superstitious players are motivated by a desire to pay tribute to the gods of fortune, in the hopes that such tokes will be returned bounteously. This conduct can only be described as an involved and intensely interested act. Moreover, the regularity of the tokes, the equal division of them by the dealers, and the daily amount received indicate that a reasonable dealer would regard them like wages. Therefore, the tokes constitute taxable income, and Olk (P) is not entitled to his refund. Reversed.

EDITOR'S ANALYSIS: Ordinary tips, like tokes, are includable in income based on the assumption that they are payments for services rendered. However, the government has long struggled with the problem of enforcement with regard to the reporting of such receipts. Section 6053 of the Internal Revenue Code requires restaurants and bars employing more than ten people to adhere to a stringent set of rules and filing requirements concerning actual or putative tip income.

NOTES:

Notes

CHAPTER 6
SCHOLARSHIPS AND PRIZES

QUICK REFERENCE RULES OF LAW

1. **Scholarships and Prizes.** When an employee receives property as part of his compensation wages, it is the fair market value of property which must be reported as gross income, not the cost of the property to the employer. (McCoy v. Commissioner)

   [For more information on valuation of property, see Casenote Law Outline on Federal Income Taxation, Chapter 3, § I, No Requirement That Income Must Take the Form of Cash.]

2. **Scholarships and Prizes.** A salary received by an employee on educational leave from an employer is not excludable from gross income as a scholarship or fellowship grant. (Bingler v. Johnson)

   [For more information on scholarships, see Casenote Law Outline on Federal Income Taxation, Chapter 3, § V, Exclusions from Gross Income.]

Notes

McCOY v. COMMISSIONER

38 T.C. 841 (1962), acq.

NATURE OF CASE: Action contesting the valuation of income received in the form of an automobile.

FACT SUMMARY: After McCoy (P) won a new car from his employer which he then traded in for cash and a different vehicle, he reported the value of the cash and trade-in car on his taxes.

CONCISE RULE OF LAW: When an employee receives property as part of his compensation wages, it is the fair market value of property which must be reported as gross income, not the cost of the property to the employer.

FACTS: During 1956, McCoy (P) worked for a division of General Electric. The company had annual sales contests, and McCoy (P) was a winner in the 1956 contest. His prize was a new 1957 Lincoln Capri two-door coupe. The cost of the vehicle to General Electric was $4,452.54. Within ten days of receiving the car, McCoy (P) traded it to a dealer for $1,000 in cash and a 1957 Ford Country Squire station wagon with a dealer price of $2,600. McCoy (P) reported $3,600 — the station wagon plus $1,000 — in his 1956 adjusted gross income. However, General Electric submitted to the IRS (D) an information return in which it reported additional compensation to McCoy (P) in the amount of $4,452.54. This was the cost to GE for the Lincoln. A deficiency in McCoy's (P) reported taxes was assessed by the IRS (D). McCoy (P) then filed suit in Tax Court, contesting the deficiency.

ISSUE: If an employee receives property as part of his compensation wages, is it the cost of the property to the employer which must be reported as gross income?

HOLDING AND DECISION: (Court) No. When an employee receives property as part of his compensation wages, it is the fair market value of property which must be reported as gross income, not the cost of the property to the employer. Were an employer to pay twice the market value for property then transferred to an employee as compensation for services, the employee would not be expected to declare the inflated price as the amount by which his gross income was increased. Similarly, if property transferred to an employee loses value during the course of the transfer, it seems unreasonable to tax a gain that the employee did not realize. In this case, McCoy (P) received a car as a bonus for sales. It is well established that cars immediately lose resale value when purchased. Even if McCoy (P), who received the car in new condition, had not driven it at all, but instead attempted to sell it immediately, he most certainly could not have sold the car for the purchase price. Driving the car to the point of sale further diminished its value. In this instance, neither the price paid by General Electric nor the price received by McCoy (P) determines the fair market value of the car at the time McCoy (P) received it. The value of the car was reduced when taken into possession by General Electric, and again when it was driven by McCoy (P). Since there is no clear evidence as to the value at each of these times, a fair market value of $3,900 will be applied, falling between the $4,452.54 purchase price and the $3,600 disposition at resale.

EDITOR'S ANALYSIS: Regulations require that income from noncash awards be assessed at fair market value. However, determining fair market value for some goods can be difficult. Generally, the determination is an evidentiary problem, but in this case, with insufficient evidence as to fair market value, the court made a best guess.

[For more information on valuation of property, see Casenote Law Outline on Federal Income Taxation, Chapter 3, § I, No Requirement That Income Must Take the Form of Cash.]

NOTES:

BINGLER v. JOHNSON

394 U.S. 741 (1969).

NATURE OF CASE: Review of decision by court of appeals, reversing a district court ruling denying a taxpayer claim for a refund.

FACT SUMMARY: Employees (P) at Westinghouse took part in a program whereby they would receive a portion of their regular salary while working and going to school for advanced degrees, but they took exception when Westinghouse withheld taxes from the salary paid while they were in school.

CONCISE RULE OF LAW: A salary received by an employee on educational leave from an employer is not excludable from gross income as a scholarship or fellowship grant.

FACTS: Westinghouse offered a program to employees (P) which promoted completion of doctoral degrees. In the first phase of the program, employees (P) would work a regular job at Westinghouse while attending classes, but they would receive eight hours a week of "release time." Tuition remuneration was provided to the employees (P). The second phase of the program offered the employees (P) an educational leave of absence to complete a doctoral dissertation. During that time, a living stipend was paid by Westinghouse to the employees (P). To receive the program benefits, employees (P) had to agree to return to work at Westinghouse for at least two years. Westinghouse withheld taxes from the amounts paid to employees (P) in the educational program. The employees (P), including Johnson (P), filed claims for refunds, but they were denied. They then filed suit in district court. The jury decided against the employee taxpayers (P), but on appeal, the court of appeals reversed the decision. The IRS (D) sought certiorari from the Supreme Court, which granted review.

ISSUE: Is a salary received by an employee on educational leave from an employer excludable from gross income as a scholarship or fellowship grant?

HOLDING AND DECISION: (Stewart, J.) No. A salary received by an employee on educational leave from an employer is not excludable from gross income as a scholarship or fellowship grant. Congress has not specifically defined what constitutes a scholarship for purposes of the tax code. However, it does not seem inconsistent with the Code to exclude from the definition of scholarship any amounts received as compensation for services performed. The exclusion of scholarships and fellowships from gross income was merely a recognition by Congress that these two categories were special, rather than an attempt by Congress to exclude all income, regardless of the source, given to support a student. Here, the jury found that the amounts received by the employees (P) were compensation rather than scholarships. Such a finding is reasonable. The employees (P) were required to hold jobs during phase one, and they had to work for Westinghouse for two years following the completion of their education. Reversed.

EDITOR'S ANALYSIS: In the specific case of employer-employee scholarship programs, taxpayers have had difficulty arguing that the payments were excludable. The appearance of a *quid pro quo* between the employer and the employee has often led to the conclusion that any amounts received by employees in these programs are more properly construed as compensation, rather than scholarships. However, note that qualified tuition reduction programs, which permit children of teachers at certain universities and schools to attend at a reduced cost, are not taxable.

[For more information on scholarships, see Casenote Law Outline on Federal Income Taxation, Chapter 3, § V, Exclusions from Gross Income.]

NOTES:

CHAPTER 8*
DISCHARGE OF INDEBTEDNESS

QUICK REFERENCE RULES OF LAW

1. **Discharge of Indebtedness as Gift, Compensation, etc.** The retirement of debt by a corporation for less than face value represents a realized increase in net worth to the corporation and is therefore a taxable gain. (United States v. Kirby Lumber Co.)

   [For more information on canceled debts, see Casenote Law Outline on Federal Income Taxation, Chapter 3, § III, Realized Increase in Net Wealth (or Net Worth).]

2. **Discharge of Indebtedness as Gift, Compensation, etc.** If a taxpayer, in good faith, disputes the amount of a debt, a subsequent settlement of the dispute will be treated as the amount of debt cognizable for tax purposes. (Zarin v. Commissioner)

   [For more information on relief from payment obligations, see Casenote Law Outline on Federal Income Taxation, Chapter 3, § III, Realized Increase in Net Wealth (or Net Worth).]

***There are no cases in Chapter 7.**

Notes

UNITED STATES v. KIRBY LUMBER CO.

284 U.S. 1 (1931).

NATURE OF CASE: Suit for refund of income taxes paid.

FACT SUMMARY: Kirby Lumber (P) issued bonds at par value and then later repurchased some of them in the open market below par. The IRS (D) contended the difference between the issuing price and the repurchase price was a taxable gain to Kirby Lumber (P).

CONCISE RULE OF LAW: The retirement of debt by a corporation for less than face value represents a realized increase in net worth to the corporation and is therefore a taxable gain.

FACTS: Kirby Lumber (P) issued bonds having a par value of $12,127,000 for that amount. Later in the same year it was able to repurchase a part of the bonds for a price below par. The aggregate difference in price between the par value and repurchase price was $138,000. The IRS assessed a tax on that amount contending it was a taxable gain to Kirby Lumber (P). Kirby (P) paid the tax and sued for a refund.

ISSUE: Does retirement of debt for less than face value represent a taxable gain to a corporation?

HOLDING AND DECISION: (Holmes, J.) Yes. Section 61(a) defines gross income as gains or profits and income derived from any source whatever. The retirement of debt for less than face or issuing value represents a gain or income for the taxable year. By this transaction, Kirby (P) made available $138,000 previously offset by the bond obligations. This represented an accession to income within the popular meaning of those words and is a taxable event.

EDITOR'S ANALYSIS: The proceeds of a loan are not taxable to the borrower and the repayment of the principal is not deductible since neither transaction affects the borrower's net worth. An issue arises, however, when the liability is discharged without repayment by the borrower. Where a father relinquishes a liability from the son, this can quite properly be considered a gift of that amount and not taxable to the son. Where the debt is repaid through services rather than in cash, the debt reduction would clearly be income.

[For more information on canceled debts, see Casenote Law Outline on Federal Income Taxation, Chapter 3, § III, Realized Increase in Net Wealth (or Net Worth).]

NOTES:

ZARIN v. COMMISSIONER

916 F.2d 110 (3d Cir. 1990).

NATURE OF CASE: Appeal from tax court recognition of income from discharge of indebtedness.

FACT SUMMARY: Zarin (P) incurred $3.435 million in gambling debts at a New Jersey casino; after contesting the debt in court, he and the casino settled it for $500,000, and the Tax Commissioner assessed a deficiency based on the difference.

CONCISE RULE OF LAW: If a taxpayer, in good faith, disputes the amount of a debt, a subsequent settlement of the dispute will be treated as the amount of debt cognizable for tax purposes.

FACTS: Zarin (P) was a compulsive gambler who frequented Resorts Hotel International and held a line of credit there. As a "valued gaming patron," he had his line increased over the course of two years from $10,000 to $200,000 and above. Under this line, Zarin (P) could write a check, called a marker, and in return receive chips which could be used to gamble at the casino's tables. Although between June 1978 and December 1979, Zarin (P) incurred $2.5 million in gambling losses which he paid in full, in January 1980 he lost about $3.435 million. To pay for these losses, he wrote personal checks and counterchecks to Resorts, but they were returned dishonored. When Resorts filed a state action to collect the $3.435 million, Zarin (P) claimed the debt was unenforceable under New Jersey state regulations protecting compulsive gamblers. Resorts and Zarin (P) settled the claim for $500,000 in 1981. Although at first the Tax Commissioner assessed a deficiency based on recognition of $3.435 million of income in 1980 from larceny by trick and deception, upon challenge by Zarin (P) in the tax court the Commissioner changed the basis of his assessment to recognition of $2.935 million of income in 1981 from cancellation of indebtedness. The tax court agreed with the Commissioner on the latter ground, and Zarin (P) appealed.

ISSUE: If a taxpayer, in good faith, disputes the amount of a debt, will a subsequent settlement of the dispute be treated as the amount of debt cognizable for tax purposes?

HOLDING AND DECISION: (Cowen, C.J.) Yes. The proper approach in viewing the Resorts/Zarin (P) transaction is as a disputed debt or contested liability. Under the contested liability doctrine, if a taxpayer, in good faith, disputes the amount of a debt, a subsequent settlement of the dispute will be treated as the amount of debt cognizable for tax purposes. The excess of the original debt over the amount determined to have been due is disregarded for both loss and debt and accounting purposes. Here Zarin (P) incurred a $3.435 million debt while gambling at Resorts, but in court disputed liability on the basis of unenforceability. The subsequent settlement of $500,000 served only to fix the amount of the debt, and no income was realized or recognized. Zarin (P) could not have recognized income from cancellation of indebtedness because his debt did not satisfy the requirements of I.R.C. § 108. Section 108 requires that for a canceled debt to be recognized as income under I.R.C. § 61(a)(12), it must be one for which the taxpayer is liable, or one subject to property which the taxpayer holds. However, Zarin's (P) was unenforceable as a matter of New Jersey law, and therefore Zarin (P) could not have been held liable for it. Moreover, he did not have a debt subject to property which he held; the gambling chips which he "purchased" were not property, but a medium of exchange within the Resorts casino and a cash substitute. They were mere evidence of indebtedness which had no independent economic value outside the casino. Thus, Zarin (P) did not have income from cancellation of indebtedness both because he did not meet the requirements of I.R.C. § 108, and because the settlement of his debts represented a contested liability. Reversed.

EDITOR'S ANALYSIS: The logical underpinning for this case lies in the fact that when a taxpayer receives money as a loan he also incurs an obligation to repay the loan; thus, although the taxpayer receives an economic benefit from the receipt of funds, that receipt has no immediate tax consequences. No income is realized because there has been a "wash" by the taxpayer's taking on of an obligation. However, a taxable event occurs if part of the debt is released or forgiven, because then some of the taxpayer's assets are freed from being subject to the obligation.

[For more information on relief from payment obligations, see Casenote Law Outline on Federal Income Taxation, Chapter 3, § III, Realized Increase in Net Wealth (or Net Worth).]

NOTES:

CHAPTER 9
COMPENSATION FOR PERSONAL INJURY AND SICKNESS

QUICK REFERENCE RULES OF LAW

1. **Certain Disability Pensions.** Damage awards in tort and tort-type actions are excludable if they stem from personal injuries, i.e., those injuries that resulted from any invasion of the rights that an individual is granted by virtue of being a person in the sight of the law. (Threlkeld v. Commissioner)

   [For more information on excluding recoveries for personal injury from income, see Casenote Law Outline on Federal Income Taxation, Chapter 3, § V, Exclusions from Gross Income.]

2. **Certain Disability Pensions.** Since back-pay awards redress economic injury in the form of unpaid wages, back-pay awards received in settlement of Title VII claims are not excludable from gross income as damages received on account of personal injuries. (United States v. Burke)

   [For more information on excludability of damage awards under Title VII, see Casenote Law Outline on Federal Income Taxation, Chapter 3, § V, Exclusions from Gross Income.]

Notes

THRELKELD v. COMMISSIONER

87 T.C. 1294 (1986).

NATURE OF CASE: Suit in Tax Court seeking to have damages awarded for malicious prosecution excluded from taxable income.

FACT SUMMARY: After being awarded damages for malicious prosecution, Threlkeld (P) sought to exclude the entire damage award from reported gross income.

CONCISE RULE OF LAW: Damage awards in tort and tort-type actions are excludable if they stem from personal injuries, i.e., those injuries that resulted from any invasion of the rights that an individual is granted by virtue of being a person in the sight of the law.

FACTS: Williams filed a lawsuit against Threlkeld (P) to set aside a real estate contract on account of alleged fraud by Threlkeld (P). Threlkeld (P) prevailed and subsequently filed a lawsuit for malicious prosecution. In a written settlement agreement, $75,000 was allocated to compensate for the injury to Threlkeld's (P) professional reputation. Threlkeld (P) then sought to exclude the damage settlement from gross income. The IRS (D) assessed a deficiency, following the standing practice of differentiating between injury to personal reputation and injury to professional reputation. Threlkeld (P) filed suit in Tax Court to compel the exclusion.

ISSUE: Is it proper to exclude from taxable income those damages awarded for injury to personal reputation while not excluding damages for injury to professional reputation?

HOLDING AND DECISION: (Goffe, J.) No. Damage awards in tort and tort-type actions are excludable if they stem from personal injuries, i.e., those injuries that resulted from any invasion of the rights that an individual is granted by virtue of being a person in the sight of the law. There is no dispute that damages awarded for physical injuries are excludable from gross income. Likewise, damages for mental or emotional injuries are excludable. However, in defamation cases, and other related claims where injury to reputation is at issue, there has been a distinction made between damages received for injury to personal reputation and damages for injury to professional reputation. But the court of appeals in Roemer v. Commissioner, 716 F.2d 693 (9th Cir. 1983), soundly reasoned that no such distinction was justified under § 104(a)(2) of the Internal Revenue Code. Section 104(a)(2) provides that the amount of any damages received on account of personal injury is excludable from gross income. Thus the proper threshold question is whether or not an injury is personal. The origin and character of a damage claim will help determine if it is personal, not the consequences that result from the injury. Therefore, the essential element of an exclusion under § 104(a)(2) is that the income must derive from some sort of tort claim against the payor. In this case, the damage award was for malicious prosecution. To some degree, the award was to compensate for damage to reputation. Threlkeld (P) was essentially recovering for a species of defamation under another name. Since defamation and related torts involve an insult to the reputation that is personal to the individual, the damage award to Threlkeld (P) is sufficiently linked to personal injury to warrant exclusion. Judgment is entered for Threlkeld (P).

EDITOR'S ANALYSIS: The Tax Court's decision was upheld upon appeal. In the decision, Threlkeld v. Commissioner, 848 F.2d 81 (6th Cir. 1988), the court of appeals specifically stated that it would not follow Revenue Ruling 85-143, which maintained the distinction between injury to personal and professional reputation. The court held that the Revenue Ruling was inconsistent with Internal Revenue Code sections.

[For more information on excluding recoveries for personal injury from income, see Casenote Law Outline on Federal Income Taxation, Chapter 3, § V, Exclusions from Gross Income.]

NOTES:

UNITED STATES v. BURKE

_U.S._, 112 S. Ct 1867 (1992).

NATURE OF CASE: Review of reversal of a district court decision holding Title VII awards taxable as gross income.

FACT SUMMARY: Burke (P) and other women (P) working for the Tennessee Valley Authority settled a sex discrimination suit under Title VII, receiving back pay; however, the TVA withheld income taxes from the settlement awards.

CONCISE RULE OF LAW: Since back-pay awards redress economic injury in the form of unpaid wages, back-pay awards received in settlement of Title VII claims are not excludable from gross income as damages received on account of personal injuries.

FACTS: Burke (P) and other female employees (P) of the Tennessee Valley Authority brought an action against the TVA under Title VII, claiming sex discrimination in salaries. The women (P) sought injunctive relief and back pay. The parties ultimately settled the case. The TVA withheld income taxes on the settlement awards allocated to the employees (P). The women (P) filed a claim for refund of the withheld taxes. The IRS (D) rejected the argument that the settlement was excludable under the damages provision of § 104(a)(2) of the Internal Revenue Code. The women (P) filed suit in district court, where the IRS (D) position was upheld. On appeal, however, the court of appeals reversed, and the Supreme Court granted review to resolve conflicting judgments of the courts of appeals for the various circuits.

ISSUE: Are back-pay awards received in settlement of Title VII claims excludable from gross income as damages received on account of personal injuries?

HOLDING AND DECISION: (Blackmun, J.) No. Since back-pay awards redress economic injury in the form of unpaid wages, back-pay awards received in settlement of Title VII claims are not excludable from gross income as damages received on account of personal injuries. Section 104(a)(2) allows recoveries for personal injuries to be excluded from gross income. The proper line of inquiry to determine excludability is whether a damage award or settlement redresses a tort-like personal injury. The issue in this case is whether Title VII allows redress for a tort-like personal injury. Title VII of the Civil Rights Act of 1964 authorizes suit in a district court once administrative remedies are exhausted. The remedies available under Title VII are limited to back pay, injunctions, and other equitable relief. The primary focus of Title VII is to redress and prevent injuries of an economic character. There is no recognition under Title VII of the traditional harms associated with personal injury. While discrimination is an invidious practice that can cause, among other things, great emotional distress, Title VII does not focus upon curing those personal injury harms. The settlement in the TVA suit is properly construed as wages due, and thus not excludable under § 104(a)(2). Reversed.

EDITOR'S ANALYSIS: Whether one agrees with the majority depends in part upon whether one sees Title VII as protecting contractual rights to wages or redressing the personal injury caused by discriminatory employment practices. The underlying goal of Title VII is to inject economic disincentives into the marketplace that make discrimination an unprofitable practice. If a worker suffers the effects of discrimination in the form of lost wages, Title VII gives rise to a cause of action to recover those lost wages. Thus the employee is paid a fair wage and the employer is not forced to suffer the penalty of punitive damage award.

[For more information on excludability of damage awards under Title VII, see Casenote Law Outline on Federal Income Taxation, Chapter 3, § V, Exclusions from Gross Income.]

NOTES:

CHAPTER 10
FRINGE BENEFITS

QUICK REFERENCE RULES OF LAW

1. **Cafeteria Plans.** Cash payments, designated as meal allowances, are not excludable from gross income under § 119 of the Internal Revenue Code. (Commissioner v. Kowalski)

    [For more information on fringe benefits, see Casenote Law Outline on Federal Income Taxation, Chapter 3, § V, Exclusions from Gross Income.]

2. **Cafeteria Plans.** Where meals and lodging are provided to an employee for the primary purpose of benefiting the employer, the value of the meals and lodging is properly excluded from gross income. (Benaglia v. Commissioner)

    [For more information on fringe benefits, see Casenote Law Outline on Federal Income Taxation, Chapter 3, § V, Exclusions from Gross Income.]

3. **Cafeteria Plans.** The value of any trip that is paid by the employer or by a businessman primarily for his own benefit should be excluded from the gross income of the recipient. (United States v. Gotcher)

    [For more information on travel expenses, see Casenote Law Outline on Federal Income Taxation, Chapter 7, § I,Expenses Relating to the Production of Income as Opposed to Those Relating to Personal Consumption.]

Notes

COMMISSIONER v. KOWALSKI

434 U.S. 77 (1977).

NATURE OF CASE: Appeal from judgment that meal allowances were excludable from gross income.

FACT SUMMARY: State police troopers were given cash payments for the purpose of purchasing meals while on patrol, and they sought to exclude these payments from taxable income.

CONCISE RULE OF LAW: Cash payments, designated as meal allowances, are not excludable from gross income under § 119 of the Internal Revenue Code.

FACTS: Kowalski (P) worked as a state police trooper. In addition to a base salary in the year in question, he received an additional $1,697.54 as a meal allowance. Prior to 1949, the state had provided official meal stations. If a trooper could not eat there, he could be reimbursed for a meal purchased in a restaraunt. Under the meal allowance system, the troopers were required to stay in their assigned area, but could eat anywhere they chose. Troopers could even eat at home if it was within the assigned patrol area. Kowalski (P) sought to exlude the meal allowance payment from gross income under § 119. He filed suit seeking to enforce his interpretation. The court of appeals ruled in his favor, and the Commissioner (D) appealed to the Supreme Court.

ISSUE: Are cash payments to state police troopers, designated as meal allowances, excludable from gross income under § 119 of the Internal Revenue Code?

HOLDING AND DECISION: (Brennan, J.) No. Cash payments, designated as meal allowances, are not excludable from gross income under § 119 of the Internal Revenue Code. Section 119 covers meals furnished by employers, not cash reimbursements for meals. Congress intended the section to cover only meals furnished in kind. A great deal of confusion surrounded meal exclusions, and revisions to the Code in 1954 were an attempt to remove some of the confusion. In this case, the taxpayers argue that the payments were made for the convenience of the employer. However, the state troopers had great discretion in how the funds were used. They could eat at home if it was within the patrol area, and they could bring a meal, saving a substantial amount of the meal allowance. The purpose of the exclusion under § 119 was to protect employees that are forced to eat a meal provided by the employer at the place of employment, provided solely for the convenience of the employer. It cannot be said that a cash payment given with no requirements falls into this category. Reversed.

EDITOR'S ANALYSIS: Prior to the 1954 change to the Code, the treatment of employee meal benefits was chaotic. The doctrine of employer convenience was applied with differing results in different courts. The 1954 change attempted to remove much of this confusion while continuing to recognize employer convenience as a protected category. Generally, the 1954 changes to the Code removed any excludability of cash payments for meals.

[For more information on fringe benefits, see Casenote Law Outline on Federal Income Taxation, Chapter 3, § V, Exclusions from Gross Income.]

NOTES:

BENGALIA v. COMMISSIONER

36 B.T.A. 838 (1937).

NATURE OF CASE: Review of a deficiency finding by the Commissioner (D).

FACT SUMMARY: Bengalia (P) occupied a suite of rooms in a hotel where he was constantly on duty as the manager, but he did not report the value of the lodging as gross income.

CONCISE RULE OF LAW: Where meals and lodging are provided to an employee for the primary purpose of benefiting the employer, the value of the meals and lodging is properly excluded from gross income.

FACTS: Bengalia (P) was employed as the manager of several hotels in Honolulu. He was constantly on duty as the manager. For the proper performance of his duties as the full-time manager, the employer required that he occupy a suite of rooms in one of the motels. He was also provided meals on the premises. Bengalia (P) did not include the value of the meals or lodging in his gross income calculation, and the Commissioner (D) assessed a deficiency of $7,845 a year for the years in question. Bengalia (P) filed suit in Tax Court.

ISSUE: Are meals and lodging provided to a hotel manager expressly for the benefit of the employer properly excluded from gross income?

HOLDING AND DECISION: (Sternhagen, J.) Yes. Where meals and lodging are provided to an employee for the primary purpose of benefiting the employer, the value of the meals and lodging is properly excluded from gross income. When an employer requires that an employee reside and eat meals at a specific location, the employee loses a measure of choice for the convenience of the employer. In foregoing freedom for the convenience of the employer, the taxpayer is given the benefit of excluding the value of the meals and lodging from the calculation of gross income. In this case it is clear that residence on the hotel premises was necessary for Bengalia (P). Without a manager available on the site, proper attention to guests' needs could not be accomplished. The only way in which the duties required of Bengalia (P) could be performed was for him to reside at the hotel. Bengalia's (P) deficiency notice is vacated.

DISSENT: (Arnold, J.) Just because Bengalia (P) had to live in the hotel does not mean that he did not benefit. Had he not lived in the hotel, he would have had to provide for a place to live and meals to eat. The tax law should concern itself with the benefits acquired by the taxpayer, not the benefits to employers.

EDITOR'S ANALYSIS: The dissent makes a logically compelling argument, considering how broadly gross income has been defined in other cases. However, Congress has been content to let stand this interpretation of § 119 since the section has been left relatively unchanged. Congress did revise § 119 in 1954 because courts were inconsistent in applying it.

[For more information on fringe benefits, see Casenote Law Outline on Federal Income Taxation, Chapter 3, § V, Exclusions from Gross Income.]

NOTES:

UNITED STATES v. GOTCHER

401 F.2d 118 (5th Cir. 1968).

NATURE OF CASE: Appeal from a determination of tax liability under I.R.C. § 61.

FACT SUMMARY: The Gotchers (P) traveled to Germany on an all-expense-paid trip provided by Volkswagen, which sought to encourage investment in Volkswagen dealerships in the United States.

CONCISE RULE OF LAW: The value of any trip that is paid by the employer or by a businessman primarily for his own benefit should be excluded from the gross income of the recipient.

FACTS: Mr. and Mrs. Gotcher (P) received a $1,372.30 expense-paid, twelve-day trip to Germany from Volkswagen in order to tour the company's facilities there. Volkswagen provided the trip as part of an American sales effort to encourage purchases of Volkswagens by American dealerships. Mr. Gotcher (P) eventually became president of a dealership and owned a 50% share. The Gotchers (P) did not report the value of the trip as income. The government (D) asserted a deficiency of $356.79 plus $82.29 in interest. The Gotchers (P) paid and then sought a refund. The district court held that the value of the trip was not income, or, alternatively, was income and deductible as an ordinary business expense. The government (D) appealed.

ISSUE: Should the value of any trip that is paid by the employer or by a business man primarily for his own benefit be excluded from the gross income of the recipient?

HOLDING AND DECISION: (Thornberry, C.J.) Yes. The value of any trip that is paid by the employer or by a businessman primarily for his own benefit should be excluded from the gross income of the recipient. Section 61 defines gross income as income derived from whatever source, but exclusions from gross income are not limited to those enumerated by Sections 101-123. The "key" to Section 61 is the concept of economic gain to the taxpayer: (1) an economic gain and (2) a gain which benefits the taxpayer personally. Expense-paid items given a taxpayer-employee will not be gross income even if incidental benefit is derived therefrom if given primarily for the employer's convenience. The trip provided by Volkswagen was necessary in order to encourage investment and consisted mainly of twelve days of touring Volkswagen plants and German dealerships. Side trips were designed to demonstrate the post-war German economy. While the trip may have been pleasurable in part, its dominant purpose was business. While Mr. Gotcher (P) was not forced to go, in a business sense, he had no choice but to go. As income is "accessions of wealth over which the taxpayer has complete control," Gotcher (P) lacked control here. When an indirect economic gain is subordinate to an overall business purpose, the recipient is not taxed. Therefore, Mr. Gotcher (P) received no income. As for Mrs. Gotcher (P), the trip was primarily a vacation. Her presence served no bona fide business purpose for Mr. Gotcher (P); only when the wife's presence is necessary to the conduct of her husband's business are her expenses deductible. Thus, tax must be paid on half the value of the trip. Affirmed in part; reversed in part.

CONCURRENCE: (Brown, J.) It is not clear that the value of a wife's portion of a trip should be treated as income. Had her uncle paid for the trip, it would have been a pure gift.

EDITOR'S ANALYSIS: It is not clear what test always controls. A "dominant purpose" is arguably appropriate. However, the U.S. Tax Court has included in income an amount received by an employee to the extent that amount relieved the employee of personal expenses, T.C. 66 (1950). Where an employer allows an employee to use property without charge, the value of that use is income to the employee; e.g., providing a rent-free residence. Even so, many fringe benefits can escape taxation. Interestingly enough, when the President of the United States takes family and friends on board presidential aircraft, the value of the transportation provided those persons is considered to be income to the president based on first-class airfares.

[For more information on travel expenses, see Casenote Law Outline on Federal Income Taxation, Chapter 7, § I,Expenses Relating to the Production of Income as Opposed to Those Relating to Personal Consumption.]

NOTES:

Notes

CHAPTER 11
BUSINESS AND PROFIT-SEEKING EXPENSES

QUICK REFERENCE RULES OF LAW

1. **Section 212 Deductions.** In order to be deductible, an expense must be "ordinary" in the business area practiced by the taxpayer. (Welch v. Helvering)

   [For more information on prerequisites to deductibility of expenses, see Casenote Law Outline on Federal Income Taxation, Chapter 7, § I, Expenses Relating to the Production of Income as Opposed to Those Relating to Personal Consumption.]

2. **Section 212 Deductions.** While the determination of what constitutes "carrying on a business" requires case-by-case factual analysis, salaries and other expenses incurred in the management of personal assets are not deductible as business expenses. (Higgins v. Commissioner)

   [For more information on deductibility of expenses, see Casenote Law Outline on Federal Income Taxation, Chapter 7, § I, Expenses Relating to the Production of Income as Opposed to Those Relating to Personal Consumption.]

3. **Section 212 Deductions.** While determining what constitutes a trade or business is predominantly a case-by-case factual endeavor, an activity pursued with a full-time, good faith intention to produce income will usually qualify as a trade or business. (Commissioner v. Groetzinger)

4. **Section 212 Deductions.** Expenses incurred while seeking employment in a new trade or business are not deductible as a business expense incurred in the performance of that trade or business. (Estate of Nelson A. Rockefeller v. Commissioner)

   [For more information on business expense deductions, see Casenote Law Outline on Federal Income Taxation, Chapter 7, § I, Expenses Relating to the Production of Income as Opposed to Those Relating to Personal Consumption.]

Notes

WELCH v. HELVERING

290 U.S. 111 (1933).

NATURE OF CASE: Appeal from decision of court of appeals affirming Commissioner's (D) determination that repayment of bankrupt corporation's debts were capital expenditures.

FACT SUMMARY: A grain commission agent, Welch (P), repaid debts of the bankrupt corporation he used to work for.

CONCISE RULE OF LAW: In order to be deductible, an expense must be "ordinary" in the business area practiced by the taxpayer.

FACTS: Welch (P) felt that it would be to his advantage to repay the debts owed by a bankrupt company that he used to work for. Therefore, over a period of years he took a percentage of his income and repaid these discharged debts. Welch (P) attempted to deduct these payments from his income as ordinary and necessary business expenses. The Commissioner (D) disallowed them claiming that they were capital expenditures for reputation and goodwill. The Tax Court and court of appeals sustained the Commissioner (D).

ISSUE: May extraordinary expenditures be deducted from income as business expenses?

HOLDING AND DECISION: (Cardozo, J.) No. The repayment of these debts may have been helpful or even necessary for the development of Welch's (P) business. At least Welch (P) thought that they were important. However, in order to qualify as a deduction, the expense must also be "ordinary." While it is difficult to define, "ordinary" means that it would be accepted practice in a given segment of the business world. The mere fact that an individual conceives of a moral duty or necessity for a given expense is not determinative. It must be the normal method, based on experience, for dealing with a given situation. Since Welch's (P) actions of repaying the debts of a bankrupt company are extraordinary, to say the least, they do not qualify as an ordinary and necessary business expense. The decision of the Commissioner (D) is sustained.

EDITOR'S ANALYSIS: For an example of a decision upholding a similar taxpayer claim see Dunn and McCarthy, Inc. v. Commissioner, 139 F.2d 242 (2d Cir. 1943). In that case a corporation repaid certain employees who had lent money to the corporation's former president. The corporation was allowed the deductions on the grounds that they were made to promote and protect the taxpayer's existing business. The court held that the payments were not extraordinary and other corporations might well act in a similar manner. Welch was distinguished because it involved a new business.

[For more information on prerequisites to deductibility of expenses, see Casenote Law Outline on Federal Income Taxation, Chapter 7, § I, Expenses Relating to the Production of Income as Opposed to Those Relating to Personal Consumption.]

NOTES:

HIGGINS v. COMMISSIONER

312 U.S. 212 (1941).

NATURE OF CASE: Review of denial of a business expense deduction.

FACT SUMMARY: Higgins (P), who employed individuals and incurred substantial expenses incident to managing his properties and investments, sought a business deduction for salaries and expenses.

CONCISE RULE OF LAW: While the determination of what constitutes "carrying on a business" requires case-by-case factual analysis, salaries and other expenses incurred in the management of personal assets are not deductible as business expenses.

FACTS: Higgins (P) devoted a substantial portion of his time to the oversight of his real estate, bond, and stock investments. He hired others to assist him in this oversight, and rented office space for that purpose. Higgins (P) claimed the salaries and expenses incident to managing his investments as business deductions. The Commissioner (D) refused the deductions. Higgins (P) petitioned the Board of Tax Appeals, which upheld the Commissioner's (D) finding. Higgins (P) appealed to the court of appeals, which also affirmed. The Supreme Court granted certiorari.

ISSUE: If an individual hires employees to aide in the management of properties and personal assets, are those salaries and related expenses deductible as business expenses?

HOLDING AND DECISION: (Reed, J.) No. While the determination of what constitutes "carrying on a business," as that phrase is used in the Tax Code, requires case-by-case factual analysis, salaries and other expenses incurred in the management of personal assets are not deductible as business expenses. Not all expenses of every business transaction are deductible. Only those expenses that relate to carrying on a business may be used to offset income. It becomes a matter for factual determination when an individual claims a deduction for business expenses. In this case, Higgins (P) spent a substantial portion of time and money managing his personal investments. However, the management of personal finances does not ordinarily fall into the category of carrying on a business. It is true that greater assets require a larger investment of time to manage them, but that is the choice of the individual investor. Nothing in the facts suggests that the IRS (D) finding should be disturbed. Affirmed.

EDITOR'S ANALYSIS: Surprisingly, there is nothing in the Code or the regulations that defines or sets guidelines for identifying what is and is not a trade or business. Given that there are no guidelines, it is also surprising to find that cases that must define trade or business are very rare. The useful reach of this particular case may, however, be limited; it most likely stands only for the proposition that management of personal assets is not a trade or business, even if done with a substantial investment of time.

[For more information on deductibility of expenses, see Casenote Law Outline on Federal Income Taxation, Chapter 7, § I, Expenses Relating to the Production of Income as Opposed to Those Relating to Personal Consumption.]

NOTES:

COMMISSIONER v. GROETZINGER

480 U.S. 23 (1987).

NATURE OF CASE: Review of decision affirming that expenditures were business expenses.

FACT SUMMARY: Groetzinger (P) attempted to earn a living solely through wagering on dog races, but he suffered a net loss for the year and declared no gross winnings from gambling.

CONCISE RULE OF LAW: While determining what constitutes a trade or business is predominantly a case-by-case factual endeavor, an activity pursued with a full-time, good faith intention to produce income will usually qualify as a trade or business.

FACTS: During most of 1978, Groetzinger (P) spent sixty to eighty hours a week wagering on dog races. He hoped to earn a living from the wagering and had no other employment. He gambled solely for his own account. His efforts generated gross winnings of $70,000 on bets of $72,032, for a net loss of $2,032 on the year. After an audit, the Commissioner (D) determined that Groetzinger (P) was subject to a minimum tax because part of the gambling loss deduction to which he was entitled was an item of tax preference. Groetzinger (P) challenged the finding in Tax Court, and the Tax Court determined that he was in the trade or business of gambling, so that no part of his losses were an item of tax preference subjecting him to a minimum tax in 1978. The Commissioner (D) appealed, and the court of appeals affirmed. The Commissioner (D) petitioned to the Supreme Court for certiorari.

ISSUE: Must an individual be engaged in the selling of goods or services to properly claim that expenses have resulted from a trade or business?

HOLDING AND DECISION: (Blackmun, J.) No. While determining what constitutes a trade or business is predominantly a case-by-case factual endeavor, an activity pursued with a full-time, good faith intention to produce income will usually qualify as a trade or business. In Deputy v. DuPont, 308 U.S. 488 (1940), Justice Frankfurter suggested in his concurring opinion that an individual must hold one's self out to others as engaged in the selling of goods or services before such activity will be construed as carrying on a trade or business. However, the majority did not accept Justice Frankfurter's narrowing definition. But the search for an acceptable definition of trade or business has proved fruitless. In this instance, the Commissioner (D) argues that Justice Frankfurter's definition would add clarity to the Tax Code. But this test would apparently include virtually all activities except gambling under its umbrella. Such an expansive test is of little use in judicial proceedings. Groetzinger (P) was engaged in a diligent, regular, full-time effort to earn an income through wagering. These factors alone make a compelling case that his wagering was an attempt at earning a livelihood, not just a hobby. There seems to be no acceptable alternative to the problem of characterizing actions as trade or business related. A case-by-case, factual analysis, with certain recurring elements, shall remain the less-than-satisfactory solution until Congress sees fit to decide otherwise. Groetzinger (P), with all facts considered, was engaged in the trade of gambling, admittedly with unsuccessful results. Affirmed.

EDITOR'S ANALYSIS: The opinion in this case expressed great discomfort with the decision in Higgins v. Commissioner, 313 U.S. 212 (1941), written nearly fifty years earlier. But no better approach than a case-by-case analysis has appeared even half a century later. Perhaps what the courts fear most is a test based entirely on common sense.

NOTES:

ESTATE OF NELSON A. ROCKEFELLER v. COMMISSIONER

762 F.2d 264 (2nd Cir. 1985).

NATURE OF CASE: Appeal from a decision of the Tax Court finding a deficiency in taxes.

NOTES:

FACT SUMMARY: Rockefeller (P) incurred expenses in connection with confirmation hearings following nomination to the position of Vice President, and he attempted to deduct these costs as business expenses.

CONCISE RULE OF LAW: Expenses incurred while seeking employment in a new trade or business are not deductible as a business expense incurred in the performance of that trade or business.

FACTS: Rockefeller (P) was nominated and confirmed as the Vice President of the United States. In the confirmation proceedings, he incurred expenses of $550,159.78, primarily for legal services. Prior to this nomination, he had been the governor of New York State, and had performed other public service jobs. On his taxes, Rockefeller (P) sought to deduct $63,275 in expenses for the confirmation. The Commissioner (D) denied these expenses, and Rockefeller (P) petitioned the Tax Court for review, seeking to deduct the full amount of his expenses.

ISSUE: Are expenses incurred while seeking employment in a new trade or business deductible as business expense?

HOLDING AND DECISION: (Friendly, J.) No. Expenses incurred while seeking employment in a new trade or business are not deductible as a business expense incurred in the performance of that trade or business. There has been substantial disagreement as to how to treat expenses incurred in seeking a new profession. Decisions have focused on the distinction between "becoming" and "being." A registered pharmacist has been held to be a different trade than that of intern pharmacist, so expenses incurred attending courses on pharmacology were not deductible. Applying such a distinction to this case, it is evident that Rockefeller (P) has not engaged in anything remotely similar to being the Vice President of the United States. Defining his occupation as public service paints with far too broad a brush. Therefore, expenses incurred to become Vice President are not deductible business expenses. Affirmed.

EDITOR'S ANALYSIS: The caselaw in this area has been particularly inconsistent. In many of the cited cases, there is not a clear majority espousing a single approach to the problem of expenses incurred in changing trades. When pluralities are cited as authority, it is clear that this area of law has room for development and harmonization.

[For more information on business expense deductions, see Casenote Law Outline on Federal Income Taxation, Chapter 7, § I, Expenses Relating to the Production of Income as Opposed to Those Relating to Personal Consumption.]

CHAPTER 12
CAPITAL EXPENDITURES

QUICK REFERENCE RULES OF LAW

1. **Capital Expenditures.** Expenses incurred in stock appraisal litigation are nondeductible expenses incident to the acquisition of capital. (Woodward v. Commissioner)

   [For more information on capital expenditures and expenses, see Casenote Law Outline on Federal Income Taxation, Chapter 6, § I, Distinguishing Capital Expenditures from Expenses.]

2. **Capital Expenditures.** Depreciation allocable to the use of taxpayer-owned equipment in the construction of capital improvements must be capitalized and recovered over the useful life of the asset constructed. (Commissioner v. Idaho Power Co.)

   [For more information on depreciation, see Casenote Law Outline on Federal Income Taxation, Chapter 5, § I, Depreciation and Depletion.]

3. **Capital Expenditures.** A structural change which does not increase the useful life or use of a building and which is the normal method of dealing with a given problem is a "repair" for tax purposes. (Midland Empire Packing Company v. Commissioner)

   [For more information on outlays for repairs vs. improvements, see Casenote Law Outline on Federal Income Taxation, Chapter 6, § I, Distinguishing Capital Expenditures From Expenses.]

4. **Capital Expenditures.** In determining if something was a business expense or a capital expenditure, the decisive test is the character of the transaction that gave rise to the expense. (Mt. Morris Drive-In Theatre Co. v. Commissioner)

   [For more information on capital expenditures, see Casenote Law Outline on Federal Income Taxation, Chapter 6, § I, Distinguishing Capital Expenditures from Expenses.]

5. **Capital Expenditures.** Premiums prepaid for insurance over a multiyear period are capital expenditures, and may be deducted only on a pro rata basis. (Commissioner v. Boylson Market Association)

   [For more information on capital expenditures and expenses, see Casenote Law Outline on Federal Income Taxation, Chapter 6, § I, Distinguishing Capital Expenditures from Expenses.]

NOTES

WOODWARD v. COMMISSIONER

397 U.S. 572 (1970).

NATURE OF CASE: Review of Tax Court decision holding expenses incurred upon appraisal of stocks to be non-deductible capital aquisition costs.

FACT SUMMARY: Taxpayers holding stock entered into litigation to appraise the company stock so that minority shareholders could be bought out when a dispute arose about continuing the company charter.

CONCISE RULE OF LAW: Expenses incurred in stock appraisal litigation are nondeductible expenses incident to the acquisition of capital.

FACTS: Woodward (P) and other taxpayers owned a majority of stock in the Telegraph-Herald. A majority of shares were voted to perpetuate the charter, which had expired. A minority voted against the extension. Iowa law required the majority voting for the renewal to purchase the minority shares at real value. Negotiations on the value of the stock failed. An appraisal action was brought in state court. A value was fixed for the shares. During the litigation, the taxpayers spent $25,000 for services in connection with the litigation. They then sought to deduct this amount as ordinary expenses paid to maintain and manage income-producing property. The Commissioner (D) denied the deduction. The Tax Court and the court of appeals affirmed the Commissioner's (D) finding. The taxpayers appealed to the Supreme Court.

ISSUE: Are expenses incurred in stock appraisal litigation deductible as ordinary and necessary expenses for management and maintenance of property held for the production of income?

HOLDING AND DECISION: (Marshall, J.) No. Expenses incurred in stock appraisal litigation are nondeductible expenses incident to the acquisition of capital. Since the inception of the federal income tax in 1913, capital expenditures have not been deductible. It is also long settled that expenses incurred in the acquisition or disposition of a capital asset are also treated as captial expenditures. An example is the brokerage fee for the purchase and sale of securities. This court has, in the past, chosen to examine the relationship out of which the expenses arose to determine how costs were to be characterized. In this case, the litigation arose from a disagreement as to how to value capital assets. Inherent in owning capital is the risk that such a disagreement will arise. Establishing the purchase price of stock clearly falls within the scope of acquisition activities. Affirmed.

EDITOR'S ANALYSIS: Underlying this decision is an economic principle of risk placement. The effect of the decision is to place the risk of litigation costs upon the stockholder, rather than allowing the risk to be shifted to other taxpayers. As a matter of equity, it is fair to place the benefits and costs with the same party.

[For more information on capital expenditures and expenses, see Casenote Law Outline on Federal Income Taxation, Chapter 6, § I, Distinguishing Capital Expenditures from Expenses.]

NOTES:

Not ordinary + necessary

COMMISSIONER v. IDAHO POWER CO.

418 U.S. 1 (1974).

NATURE OF CASE: Appeal from allowance of a depreciation deduction.

NOTES:

FACT SUMMARY: Idaho Power Co. (P) attempted to take a deduction for depreciation on equipment it owned and used in the construction of improvements and additions to its capital facilities.

CONCISE RULE OF LAW: Depreciation allocable to the use of taxpayer-owned equipment in the construction of capital improvements must be capitalized and recovered over the useful life of the asset constructed.

FACTS: An accrual basis taxpayer and public utility, the Idaho Power Co. (P) used some equipment it owned in the construction of improvements and additions to its capital facilities. It claimed as a deduction from gross income all the year's depreciation on such equipment, including that portion attributable to its use in constructing capital facilities. The Commissioner (D) disallowed the deduction for the construction-related depreciation, claiming it was a nondeductible capital expenditure but allowing it to be amortized and deducted over the useful life of the related capital asset. The tax court agreed. The court of appeals held that normal depreciation rules applied and allowed depreciation to be taken over the life of the equipment.

ISSUE: Must the depreciation allocable to the use of equipment in constructing capital improvements be capitalized and recovered over the useful life of the asset constructed?

HOLDING AND DECISION: (Blackmun, J.) Yes. That part of equipment depreciation that is allocable to its use in constructing capital improvements must be capitalized and recovered over the useful life of the asset constructed. The investment in the equipment is assimilated into the cost of the capital asset it constructed and is not at an end when the equipment itself is exhausted. Such capital expenditures are not deductible from current income according to I.R.C. § 263. Reversed.

EDITOR'S ANALYSIS: Among the costs of constructing capital assets is the interest paid on the construction funds and the real estate taxes. Until 1976, such costs were allowed as a current deduction even though they are as tied-in to the capital asset as the depreciation in this case. In that year, I.R.C. § 189 was adopted, providing that such costs be charged to capital account and amortized over ten years rather than currently deducted.

[For more information on depreciation, see Casenote Law Outline on Federal Income Taxation, Chapter 5, § I, Depreciation and Depletion.]

MIDLAND EMPIRE PACKING CO.

T.C., 14 T.C. 635 (1950).

NATURE OF CASE: Appeal from Commissioner's (D) decision holding that the oil-proofing of a basement was a capital improvement.

FACT SUMMARY: Midland Empire Packing (P) oil-proofed its basement to protect against oil seepage from a nearby refinery.

CONCISE RULE OF LAW: A structural change which does not increase the useful life or use of a building and which is the normal method of dealing with a given problem is a "repair" for tax purposes.

FACTS: Midland Empire Packing (P) used its basement for curing hides. After using it for this purpose for 25 years, Midland (P) discovered that oil seepage was occurring from a nearby refinery. The basement was oil-proofed and Midland (P) attempted to deduct the oil-proofing as an ordinary and necessary business expense. The Commissioner (D) denied the deduction claiming that it was a capital improvement and should be depreciated.

ISSUE: Should a structural change which does not add to the life or use of a building, and is the normal manner of dealing with a specific situation, be capitalized?

HOLDING AND DECISION: (Arundell, J.) No. A repair merely serves to keep property in an operating condition over the probable life of the property and for the purpose for which it was used. It adds nothing of value to the property, merely maintains it. Section 162 permits deductions for ordinary and necessary business expenses. While the Commissioner (D) concedes that the oil-proofing was necessary, he claimed that it was not an ordinary expense. Ordinary does not mean that an expense must be habitual. It merely requires that, based on experience, the expense would be a common and accepted means of combating a given problem. Here, neither the life nor use of the basement was changed. Certainly oil-proofing is the normal means of combating oil seepage. The fact that the problem did not exist for 25 years is not determinative. Once it occurred, Midland (P) dealt with it in a normal and acceptable manner. The oil-proofing was a repair rather than a capital improvement. The Commissioner's (D) decision is overturned.

EDITOR'S ANALYSIS: Hotel Sulgrave, Inc. v. Commissioner, 21 T.C. 619 (1954), held that the addition of a sprinkler system, even though ordered by the State, was a capital improvement. The court held that while it did not extend the use or life of the hotel, it made the property more valuable for use in petitioner's business through its compliance with state requirements.

[For more information on outlays for repairs vs. improvements, see Casenote Law Outline on Federal Income Taxation, Chapter 6, § I, Distinguishing Capital Expenditures From Expenses.]

NOTES:

MT. MORRIS DRIVE-IN THEATRE CO.

25 T.C. 272 (1955).

NATURE OF CASE: Appeal from disallowance of a business expense deduction.

FACT SUMMARY: The way in which the land was cleared in building the Mt. Morris Drive-In Theatre (P) caused an increase in drainage, so a drainage system was installed under threat of litigation from a neighbor.

CONCISE RULE OF LAW: In determining if something was a business expense or a capital expenditure, the decisive test is the character of the transaction that gave rise to the expense.

FACTS: Knowing the land on which it was building sloped toward one particular corner of the neighboring land owned by Nickolas, Mt. Morris (P) went ahead and built a drive-in theatre. In so doing, it removed the covering vegetation from the land, increased its grade, and thereby increased the water drainage onto Nickolas' land. When it rained, there was a flooding of the Nickolas land and trailer park, so a suit was filed for the damage and for an injunction. Seeking to end the possibility of any future suit, Mt. Morris (P) settled the suit by agreeing to, and constructing, a drainage system. The Commissioner (D) disallowed the taking of a business deduction for the cost, claiming it was a capital expenditure. The tax court agreed.

ISSUE: Does the character of the transaction that gave rise to an expense determine whether it constitutes a deductible business expense or a capital expenditure?

HOLDING AND DECISION: (Kern, J.) Yes. The decisive test in determining if something constitutes a business expense or a capital expenditure is the character of the transaction that gave rise to the expense. Here, it was obvious from the beginning that a drainage system would be required and that until this was accomplished, the capital investment was incomplete. The cost of its construction was really a part of the process of completing the initial investment in the land for its intended use, so the transaction was a capital expenditure and gave rise to no business deduction.

CONCURRENCE: (Raum, J.) This expenditure for drainage would clearly have been capital in character if made when the theater was initially built, and that does not change simply because it was made later.

DISSENT: (Rice, J.) This expenditure did not improve, better, extend, increase, or prolong the property's useful life nor cure the geological defect. It merely dealt with that defect's immediate consequences. Thus, I cannot agree that the expenditure was capital in nature.

EDITOR'S ANALYSIS: In a number of cases, an undetected geological defect caused problems the taxpayer had to remedy. Courts have allowed such expenditures to be treated as business expenses. The main difference in this case is that the problem was foreseeable when construction began.

[For more information on capital expenditures, see Casenote Law Outline on Federal Income Taxation, Chapter 6, § I, Distinguishing Capital Expenditures from Expenses.]

NOTES:

COMMISSIONER v. BOYLSTON MARKET ASSOCIATION

131 F.2d 966 (1st Cir. 1942).

NATURE OF CASE: Review of decision denying an expense deduction for insurance premiums.

FACT SUMMARY: A taxpayer prepaid insurance for several years and then sought to deduct the full amount paid as a business expense in the first year.

CONCISE RULE OF LAW: Premiums prepaid for insurance over a multiyear period are capital expenditures, and may be deducted only on a pro rata basis.

FACTS: A taxpayer paid for a multiyear insurance policy in full in the first year. He then sought to deduct the entire cost of the premium as a business expense in the first year. The Commissioner (D) denied the deduction. The taxpayer filed suit, and the Tax Court upheld the Commissioner (D). The decision was appealed to the court of appeals.

ISSUE: When a taxpayer prepays an insurance premium for a several-year period, may he then deduct the full amount of the premium as a business expense during the first year?

HOLDING AND DECISION: (Mahoney, J.) No. Premiums pre-paid for insurance over a multiyear period are capital expenditures, and may be deducted only on a pro rata basis. A multiyear insurance policy has a life expectancy greater than one year. Its value extends beyond the tax year in question. To permit a taxpayer to deduct the cost of its acquisition in a single year would distort the income of the taxpayer. An allocation over the life expectancy of the asset prevents the distortion. In this case, the insurance policy is like any other investment having a lifespan greater than a year. It is logically equivalent to a lease or other such asset. Affirmed.

EDITOR'S ANALYSIS: The court in this case was also reacting to the problem of early cancellation of the policy. It would be difficult to identify when a taxpayer had canceled a policy before the planned expiration date. A pro rata refund would issue from the insurance company, and it seems logically consistent to require the deductions to parallel the rebate structure for a policy canceled early.

[For more information on capital expenditures and expenses, see Casenote Law Outline on Federal Income Taxation, Chapter 6, § I, Distinguishing Capital Expenditures from Expenses.]

NOTES:

Notes

CHAPTER 13
DEPRECIATION

QUICK REFERENCE RULES OF LAW

1. **Depreciation.** A taxpayer seeking a depreciation deduction bears the burden of proving that an asset has a determinable useful life. (Associated Obstetricians & Gynecologists, P.C. v. Commissioner)

   [For more information on prerequisites for depreciation, see Casenote Law Outline on Federal Income Taxation, Chapter 5, § I, Depreciation and Depletion.]

Notes

ASSOCIATED OBSTETRICIANS & GYNECOLOGISTS, P.C. v. COMMISSIONER

T.C.M. 1983-380 (1983), aff'd 762 F.2d 38 (6th Cir. 1985).

NATURE OF CASE: Tax Court Memo denying a depreciation adjustment to tax basis.

FACT SUMMARY: A medical group (P) purchased numerous works of art to decorate new facilities and then claimed depreciation deductions on the artwork.

CONCISE RULE OF LAW: A taxpayer seeking a depreciation deduction bears the burden of proving that an asset has a determinable useful life.

FACTS: Associated Obstetricians & Gynecologists (P) was organized by Caldwell to operate a medical office and practice in the obstetrics and gynecology branch of medicine. In 1974, AOG (P) moved to a new office. From 1973 to 1977, AOG (P) purchased over seventy works of art to decorate the new office. The total cost of the artwork acquired was $75,410.32. AOG (P) listed the artworks on its depreciation schedule and claimed deductions during the tax years at issue. Useful lives of ten years were selected for a majority of the art, the same period that was applied to office furniture and medical equipment. In a deficiency notice, the Commissioner (D) determined that the amounts of $5,748.30 and $8,004.45 claimed in 1976 and 1977, respectively, as depreciation on art objects were not allowable because the useful lives of works of art had not been established. AOG (P) petitioned the Tax Court as to the permissibility of the depreciation deductions.

ISSUE: Does a taxpayer bear the responsibility of showing that an asset has a determinable useful life so as to allow depreciation?

HOLDING AND DECISION: (Court) Yes. A taxpayer seeking a depreciation deduction bears the burden of proving that an asset has a determinable useful life. Deductions are matters of legislative grace, and a taxpayer seeking a deduction must show that the deduction satisfies the requirements of an applicable statute. Thus a finding by the IRS (D) of a deficiency is presumed correct until proven to be in error. If an asset is determined not to have a determinable useful life, the taxpayer must offer sufficient evidence that a determinable useful life exists to overcome the finding by the IRS (D). In this case, AOG (P) attempted to depreciate works of art. The Commissioner (D) determined that art does not generally have a determinable useful life because the physical condition of the art will not usually limit or determine its useful life. And AOG (P) was noncommittal concerning the length of time that the art would be displayed, or what might be the final disposition of the pieces. The vague evidence of expected life offered by AOG (P) does not sustain their burden of proof. Judgment for the Commissioner (D).

EDITOR'S ANALYSIS: This case illustrates a procedural hurdle the taxpayer must overcome in claiming a depreciation deduction. While many assets are specifically listed in Treasury regulations, not all tangible assets are listed, or are only listed contingent upon their use. A taxpayer must be certain that evidence of the useful life of an asset is available should a deduction be challenged.

[For more information on prerequisites for depreciation, see Casenote Law Outline on Federal Income Taxation, Chapter 5, § I, Depreciation and Depletion.]

NOTES:

Notes

CHAPTER 14
LOSSES AND BAD DEBTS

QUICK REFERENCE RULES OF LAW

1. **Losses and Bad Debts.** Mere offers to rent as well as sell a personal residence are insufficient to provide the necessary foundation for the deduction of a loss incurred in a transaction entered into for profit, as required by § 165(c)(2). (Cowles v. Commissioner)

   [For more information on conversion of assets from personal to business use, see Casenote Law Outline on Federal Income Taxation, Chapter 7, § I, Expenses Relating to the Production of Income as Opposed to Those Relating to Personal Consumption.]

2. **Losses and Bad Debts.** A taxpayer, attempting to deduct funds lent to a corporation as a business bad debt, must establish that the dominant motivation for the original transaction involved a business purpose. (United States v. Generes)

   [For more information on "primary purpose" test, see Casenote Law Outline on Federal Income Taxation, Chapter 7, § I, Expenses Relating to the Production of Income.]

Notes

COWLES v. COMMISSIONER

T.C.M. 1970-198 (1970).

NATURE OF CASE: Tax Court Memo denying a deduction for losses under § 165(c)(2) of the Tax Code.

FACT SUMMARY: The Cowleses (P) listed their personal residence for sale or rent, and then claimed a loss on the eventual sale as a tax deduction.

CONCISE RULE OF LAW: Mere offers to rent as well as sell a personal residence are insufficient to provide the necessary foundation for the deduction of a loss incurred in a transaction entered into for profit, as required by § 165(c)(2).

FACTS: The Cowleses (P) acquired real property that they used as a residence from 1958 until June 1964. Mr. Cowles (P) was transferred to another city, so the Cowleses (P) contracted with real estate brokers to sell their house. On July 28, 1964, some three months later, the Cowleses (P) contracted with other real estate brokers for their services in renting as well as selling the residence. Two offers to rent were received; one was rejected as too low, and the other was withdrawn. On October 11, 1966, the residence sold for $26,000. The Cowles's (P) cost basis in the home was $34,745. The Cowleses (P) listed the loss on the sale as a deduction under § 165(c)(2). The deduction was rejected by the Commissioner (D) of the IRS. The Cowleses (P) initiated an action in Tax Court to have their deduction reinstated.

ISSUE: Are offers to rent as well as sell a personal residence sufficient to provide the necessary foundation for the deduction of a loss incurred in a transaction entered into for profit, as required by § 165(c)(2)?

HOLDING AND DECISION: (Tannenwald, J.) No. Mere offers to rent as well as sell a personal residence are insufficient to provide the necessary foundation for the deduction of a loss incurred in a transaction entered into for profit, as required by § 165(c)(2). This case poses a difficult conceptual problem. The Commissioner (D) concedes that an offer to rent a property is sufficient to allow certain deductions under §§ 167 and 212, which define holding a property for the production of income. This is a long-supported position in decided cases. However, offering a property for rent is insufficient to permit a holding that the property is "otherwise appropriated to income-producing purposes" within the meaning of § 1.165-9 of the Income Tax Regulations. Essentially, the case law has established that if the property was originally procured to use as a personal residence, an offer to rent as well as sell is insufficient to hold that the transaction was entered into for profit. And such a holding is necessary if a loss on the sale is to be deducted pursuant to § 165(c)(2). While it seems odd that an offer to rent will permit the deduction of some expenses associated with holding a property for the production of income, but won't permit the deduction of a loss on the sale, that is long-established case law. The Commissioner's (D) denial of the deduction is upheld.

EDITOR'S ANALYSIS: Individuals will have trouble reconciling this inconsistent position in the Code and the Regulations in their favor. Real property acquired originally as a residence simply maintains the character of a personal expenditure, even when offered for rent. Substantial steps and a sufficient length of time would probably be necessary to change the character of a property to that of a profit-seeking business.

[For more information on conversion of assets from personal to business use, see Casenote Law Outline on Federal Income Taxation, Chapter 7, § I, Expenses Relating to the Production of Income as Opposed to Those Relating to Personal Consumption.]

NOTES:

U.S. v. GENERES

405 U.S. 93 (1972).

NATURE OF CASE: Appeal by Commissioner (D) from decisions holding that transaction was a business debt rather than a non-business one.

FACT SUMMARY: Generes (P) attempted to deduct funds paid by him, under the terms of an indemnification agreement of a corporation which became insolvent, as a business bad debt.

CONCISE RULE OF LAW: A taxpayer, attempting to deduct funds lent to a corporation as a business bad debt, must establish that the dominant motivation for the original transaction involved a business purpose.

FACTS: Generes (P) and his son-in-law formed an equal partnership in a construction business. As the business became successful they incorporated. Generes (P) owned 44 percent of the stock and was the corporation's president. He received $12,000 a year for 6 to 8 hours a week's work. Generes (P) also held a full-time position as president of a savings and loan. His average yearly income totaled $40,000. He and his son-in-law signed a surety agreement indemnifying a lender from loss on loans made to the corporation for its construction projects. The corporation seriously underbid two projects and Generes (P) had to pay $162,000 to the lender under the agreement. Generes (P) filed a net operating loss carry-back for this amount on the basis that this was a business bad debt as provided for under § 172. The Commissioner (D) denied the carry-back deduction on the basis that this was a non-business bad debt on which only a short-term capital loss could be claimed. A jury trial was held and the jury was instructed, over the government's objection, that a debt is proximately related to a taxpayer's trade or business where a significant reason for the incurrence of the debt was business motivated. The government appealed claiming that the business motivation must have been the dominant reason for the debt. Cert. was granted because of a split between the circuits.

ISSUE: Where a business purpose is secondary to a nonbusiness purpose for lending funds to a corporation, can the taxpayer claim a business bad debt deduction when it later becomes worthless?

HOLDING AND DECISION: (Blackburn, J.) No. The proper test to be applied to situations in which the taxpayer may have both business and non-business motives for the transaction is what was his dominant/primary reason for the loan. Here, Generes (P) was both a shareholder in the corporation (a non-business purpose) and an officer in it (business purpose). It must be determined whether his actions were to primarily protect his investment or were to further the business of the corporation. The Code carefully distinguishes between business and non-business losses, expenses and bad debt and provides for differing tax treatment. Since this evidences a Congressional intent that they be treated differently, any test applied must be meaningful. If only a "significant motive" test were applied, it would do little to differentiate between business and non-business motives. The "dominant motive" test provides guidelines of certainty for the triers of fact. We find that, based on the evidence adduced at trial, that Generes' (P) dominant motivation was non-business. He claimed that he signed the agreement to protect his job and gave no thought to his $38,900 capital investment. In light of Generes' (P) tax bracket, this would mean that his $12,000 salary might net him $7,000. It is less than 1/5 of his capital contribution. As well as not establishing his motivation except through self-serving testimony, it is unlikely that a taxpayer would incur the potential liability accepted by Generes (P) to protect this amount of salary, especially in light of his other income. For these reasons we reverse and hold that the taxpayer's dominant motive was non-business.

EDITOR'S ANALYSIS: In A.J. Whipple, 373 U.S. 193 (1963) a taxpayer made loans to several corporations in which he was a major shareholder. He also sold equipment on credit and leased property to these corporations. These debts were held to be non-business. Whipple was considered to be acting as an investor. A partially worthless business debt may be deducted to the extent charged off by the business, but a non-business bad debt must be totally worthless before a deduction will be allowed. § 166(a)(2).

[For more information on "primary purpose" test, see Casenote Law Outline on Federal Income Taxation, Chapter 7, § I, Expenses Relating to the Production of Income.]

NOTES:

CHAPTER 15
TRAVEL EXPENSES

QUICK REFERENCE RULES OF LAW

1. **Travel Expenses.** A taxpayer traveling on business may deduct the cost of his meals only if his trip requires him to stop for rest or sleep. (United States v. Correll)

   [For more information on tax treatment of meals and lodging, see Casenote Law Outline on Federal Income Taxation, Chapter 7, § I, Expenses Relating to the Production of an Income.]

2. **Travel Expenses.** If the temporary job does not necessitate the maintenance of two residences, then living and travel outlays incident to the temporary job are not deductible as expenses incurred away from home. (Hantzis v. Commissioner)

   [For more information on travel expenses, see Casenote Law Outline on Federal Income Taxation, Chapter 7, § I, Expenses Relating to the Production of Income as Opposed to Those Relating to Personal Consumption.]

3. **Travel Expenses.** If a taxpayer maintains two residences to facilitate operation of two geographically separated businesses, § 162(a)(2) allows deductions for duplicate living expenses incurred at the minor post of duty. (Andrews v. Commissioner)

   [For more information on travel and lodging expenses, see Casenote Law Outline on Federal Income Taxation, Chapter 7, § I, Expenses Relating to the Production of Income as Opposed to Those Relating to Personal Consumption.]

4. **Travel Expenses.** Revenue Ruling 90-23 permits deductions for transportation between the taxpayer s residence and temporary job sites if the taxpayer also has one or more regular job sites, which, if appropriate, may be the taxpayer s residence. (Walker v. Commissioner)

   [For more information on travel expenses, see Casenote Law Outline on Federal Income Taxation, Chapter 7, § I, Expenses Relating to the Production of Income as Opposed to Those Relating to Personal Consumption.]

Notes

UNITED STATES v. CORRELL

389 U.S. 299 (1967).

NATURE OF CASE: Appeal from a determination of tax liability under I.R.C. § 162 (a)(2).

FACT SUMMARY: Correll (P), a traveling salesman, sought to deduct as a business expense the cost of breakfast and lunch eaten on the road, although he ate dinner every night at home.

CONCISE RULE OF LAW: A taxpayer traveling on business may deduct the cost of his meals only if his trip requires him to stop for rest or sleep.

FACTS: Correll (P) was a traveling salesman for a wholesale grocery company. He would eat breakfast and lunch on the road and return home in time for dinner. Correll (P) deducted the cost of breakfast and lunch as a travel expense incurred in the pursuit of business "while away from home" under § 162(a)(2). Because his travels required neither rest nor sleep, the Government (D) disallowed the deduction, ruling it to be a personal expense under § 262. After Correll (P) paid his assessed tax deficiency and sued successfully for a refund in district court, which the Sixth Circuit Court affirmed, the Government (D) appealed.

ISSUE: May a taxpayer traveling on business deduct the cost of his meals only if his trip requires him to stop for rest or sleep?

HOLDING AND DECISION: (Stewart, J.) Yes. A taxpayer traveling on business may deduct the cost of his meals only if his trip requires him to stop for rest or sleep. The Government (D) has long interpreted the limiting phrase "away from home" to exclude all trips not requiring rest or sleep regardless of how many cities visited or miles covered in a single day. The Government's (D) view allows for easy application by placing all-day travelers in the same position. The statute speaks of "meals and lodging" as a unit to be had away from home which suggests an overnight stay must be made. Reversed.

EDITOR'S ANALYSIS: Where a taxpayer was not away from home overnight but stopped his car by the roadside for naps, his deduction for the cost of his meals was disallowed. Barry v. Commissioner, 435 F.2d, 290 (1st Cir. 1970). Rev. Rul. 75-168, 1975-19 I.R.C. § 12 permits truckdrivers to deduct meal and lodging expenses during layovers of approximately eight hours which were provided for rest or sleep. However, no deduction was allowed for short, half-hour layovers. The Court admitted that the rule in Correll was somewhat arbitrary but saw no reason to distinguish between the New York to Washington, D.C. commuter who eats breakfast and dinner at home and lunch in the nation's capital and the city commuter who eats breakfast and dinner at home and lunch a block down the street from his office.

[For more information on tax treatment of meals and lodging, see Casenote Law Outline on Federal Income Taxation, Chapter 7, § I, Expenses Relating to the Production of an Income.]

NOTES:

HANTZIS v. COMMISSIONER

638 F.2d 248 (1st Cir. 1981).

NATURE OF CASE: Appeal from decision allowing travel expenses deduction.

FACT SUMMARY: A law student took a job in another city, incurring expenses, while her husband continued to reside at their home, and the couple sought to deduct the costs as travel-related business expenses.

CONCISE RULE OF LAW: If the temporary job does not necessitate the maintenance of two residences, then living and travel outlays incident to the temporary job are not deductible as expenses incurred away from home.

FACTS: Catherine Hantzis (P) was a law student in Boston. She found a law clerk position in the summer in New York. She moved to New York for ten weeks, renting an apartment, while her husband stayed at their home in Boston. She returned home occasionally for personal reasons, having no business activities in Boston. The couple sought to deduct the expense of her stay in New York on their taxes. The Commissioner (D) denied the deduction. The couple filed suit, and the Tax Court permitted the deduction. The Commissioner (D) appealed.

ISSUE: If a taxpayer accepts a temporary job in another city, are expenses incurred while away from home for the purposes of deducting under § 162(a)(2)?

HOLDING AND DECISION: (Campbell, J.) No. If the temporary job does not necessitate the maintenance of two residences, then living and travel outlays incident to the temporary job are not deductible as expenses incurred away from home. Travel expenses must be incurred away from home to be deductible. Thus, the location of the home must be fixed before the deduction can be approved or denied. In this case, Mrs. Hantzis (P) had no need to maintain a home in Boston. She had no business connection with the city of Boston. The home was kept for Mr. Hantzis, but that cannot substitute for a showing that Mrs. Hantzis (P) required the maintenance of two homes. Thus, her expenses in New York were not incurred while away from home. As a result, the expenses were not deductible. Reversed.

CONCURRENCE: (Keeton, J.) The majority has defined home in manner different from ordinary meaning. It was for personal convenience that the taxpayer maintained two residences. Thus, it cannot be said that she was away from home in pursuit of business. Her home was in New York while she was there, and the cost of keeping a home in Boston was not necessitated by business.

EDITOR'S ANALYSIS: In regard to the travel expenses deduction, the courts have made a variety of distinctions and apparently conflicting decisions. To analyze otherwise, the best one can do is identify a few major decisions and associate their fact patterns with their holdings. This case lacks pursuasiveness in its convoluted analysis of the definition of home.

[For more information on travel expenses, see Casenote Law Outline on Federal Income Taxation, Chapter 7, § I, Expenses Relating to the Production of Income as Opposed to Those Relating to Personal Consumption.]

NOTES:

ANDREWS v. COMMISSIONER

931 F.2d 132 (1st Cir. 1991).

NATURE OF CASE: Review of a Tax Court finding that travel expenses were not deductible.

FACT SUMMARY: When Andrews (P), engaged in the construction business, began a second business consisting of horse breeding, he sought to deduct travel and living expenses related to the second business, which was in another state.

CONCISE RULE OF LAW: If a taxpayer maintains two residences to facilitate operation of two geographically separated businesses, § 162(a)(2) allows deductions for duplicate living expenses incurred at the minor post of duty.

FACTS: Andrews (P) operated a seasonal swimming pool business in New England. During the off-season, he began to race and breed horses. In 1972 he moved the horse business to Florida, where it prospered. Andrews (P) was required to make an increasing number of trips to Florida because of the growing horse business. To reduce lodging and travel costs, he bought a condominium in Florida in 1976. He used the condominium in Florida as his residence during the racing season. Andrews (P) sought to deduct expenses for maintaining a duplicate residence. The Commissioner (D) denied the deductions. Andrews (P) filed suit in Tax Court, which ruled that he had two tax homes and denied the deductions. He appealed to the court of appeals.

ISSUE: If two residences are maintained to facilitate operation of two geographically separated businesses, are travel expenses and duplicate living expenses incurred as a result of the two businesses deductible?

HOLDING AND DECISION: (Campbell, J.) Yes. If a taxpayer maintains two residences to facilitate operation of two geographically separated businesses, § 162(a)(2) allows deductions for duplicate living expenses incurred at the minor post of duty. Section 162 provides a category of deductions for business expenses which reflects the principle that a person's taxable income should not include the cost of producing that income. Looking specifically at travel expenses, it has been held that they are deductible only if reasonable, incurred away from home, and incurred in pursuit of business. In this case, the Tax Court held that Andrews (P) traveled between two homes, and thus did not incur any expenses "away from home." But this court has previously held that a taxpayer who must travel to a distant second place of employment is just as much within the travel expense deduction provisions as an employee who travels at the behest of his employer. Andrews (P) was required to incur duplicate living expenses. Reasonableness requires that the "home" be located at the major post of duty. Duplicate expenses incurred at the minor post of duty are deductible. It remains to be determined, as a matter of fact, which of Andrew's (P) homes are at his major post of duty, and thus his "tax home." Vacated and remanded for further proceedings.

EDITOR'S ANALYSIS: The phrase "away from home" was at issue in this case, and surprisingly, the phrase has never been definitively interpreted by the Supreme Court. This is problematic since the lower courts and the IRS disagree as to the definition of the phrase. Most troubling is the fact that the various circuits have differed in their approaches to the situation.

[For more information on travel and lodging expenses, see Casenote Law Outline on Federal Income Taxation, Chapter 7, § I, Expenses Relating to the Production of Income as Opposed to Those Relating to Personal Consumption.]

NOTES:

WALKER v. COMMISSIONER

101 T.C. 36 (1993).

NATURE OF CASE: Action challenging IRS denial of business expense deductions.

FACT SUMMARY: Walker (P), a timber cutter, drove to numerous job sites each day to cut timber, repaired his tools in his home, and sought to deduct the entire amount of vehicle expenses as work related.

CONCISE RULE OF LAW: Revenue Ruling 90-23 permits deductions for transportation between the taxpayer's residence and temporary job sites if the taxpayer also has one or more regular job sites, which, if appropriate, may be the taxpayer's residence.

FACTS: Walker (P) drove daily from his residence to numerous job sites in the Black Hills National Forest, where he worked six to seven hours cutting trees. He also worked about seven hours a week at his residence repairing his tools. He stored his tools in his residence and took calls for jobs there as well. Walker (P) sought to deduct all his vehicle-related travel expenses, but the Commissioner (D) of the IRS allowed only 60% of the expenses. The Commissioner (D) argued that the portion of each trip to and from the cutting sites was not deductible. Walker (P) filed suit in Tax Court, seeking to deduct the full measure of his expenses.

ISSUE: If the taxpayer's residence is a regular place of business, are expenses incurred traveling to other temporary job sites deductible?

HOLDING AND DECISION: (Court) Yes. Revenue Ruling 90-23 permits deductions for transportation between the taxpayer's residence and temporary job sites if the taxpayer also has one or more regular job sites, which, if appropriate, may be the taxpayer's residence. It is well-settled that the cost of commuting between a residence and a regular place of employment is nondeductible. But transportation costs between places of business may be deductible. And if the residence is the principal place of business, then travel costs to local job sites may be deducted if the expenses are in the nature of normal business travel. In the present case, previous case law would not allow Walker (P) to receive the full measure of his expenses as a deduction, because he certainly cannot establish that his residence is his principal place of business. But Revenue Ruling 90-23 changes the analysis. The Commissioner (D) has ruled that where a taxpayer has one or more regular places of business, the expense of traveling between the residence and temporary work locations within the area is deductible. Here, Walker (P) had a regular place of business in his home. Therefore, the cost of traveling from his residence to temporary tree-cutting sites is deductible. The Revenue Ruling and the case law are inconsistent, and since the Tax Court has been forced to choose between the two, Revenue Ruling 90-23 will be seen as a concession that Walker (P) may deduct all his business travel expenses.

EDITOR'S ANALYSIS: The language of Revenue Ruling 90-23 backed the IRS into a corner. The Commissioner (D) attempted to argue that the entire Black Hills Forest was one site, and Walker's (P) commutes to different areas of the forest did not qualify as travel between different localities. The Tax Court was probably not thrilled to be forced to choose between its own case law and the Revenue Ruling. The result was an interpretation that did not favor the IRS position.

[For more information on travel expenses, see Casenote Law Outline on Federal Income Taxation, Chapter 7, § I, Expenses Relating to the Production of Income as Opposed to Those Relating to Personal Consumption.]

NOTES:

CHAPTER 16
ENTERTAINMENT AND BUSINESS MEALS

QUICK REFERENCE RULES OF LAW

1. **Entertainment and Business.** For a permissible deduction under § 274(a)(1)(A) of the Tax Code, the item must be directly related to the taxpayer's business, or, if the item directly precedes or follows a bona fide business discussion, the item must be associated with the active conduct of the taxpayer s business. (Walliser v. Commissioner)

   [For more information on business entertainment expenses, see Casenote Law Outline on Federal Income Taxation, Chapter 7, § I, Expenses Relating to the Production of Income as Opposed to Those Relating to Personal Consumption.]

2. **Entertainment and Business.** The expenses of daily business meeting lunches among coworkers are not deductible as necessary business expenses, even though the meetings might be necessary from a business perspective. (Moss v. Commissioner)

   [For more information on business expenses, see Casenote Law Outline on Federal Income Taxation, Chapter 7, § I, Expenses Relating to the Production of Income as Opposed to Those Relating to Personal Consumption.]

Notes

WALLISER v. COMMISSIONER

72 T.C. 433 (1974).

NATURE OF CASE: Suit challenging an IRS denial of certain business expense deductions.

FACT SUMMARY: Walliser (P) went abroad on tour groups in the hopes of meeting individuals interested in borrowing funds, thus enabling him to meet loan sale quotas at the bank where he worked.

CONCISE RULE OF LAW: For a permissible deduction under § 274(a)(1)(A) of the Tax Code, the item must be directly related to the taxpayer's business, or, if the item directly precedes or follows a bona fide business discussion, the item must be associated with the active conduct of the taxpayer's business.

FACTS: During the taxable years 1973 and 1974, Walliser (P) was vice president and manager of First Federal Savings & Loan Association. First Federal had loan production quotas and offered salary raises for loan output. Walliser (P) traveled abroad in tour groups for people in the building industry. The tours were arranged as guided vacations, with sightseeing and other recreation. But Walliser (P) went on the trips to meet potential customers. He believed that the tours would generate business in the form of loans at First Federal. Walliser (P) deducted the cost of the tours as employee business expenses. The IRS (D) denied the deductions, and Walliser (P) filed suit in Tax Court.

ISSUE: Are expenses incurred traveling in the hopes of meeting potential business clients deductible as business expenses?

HOLDING AND DECISION: (Tannenwald, J.) No. For a permissible deduction under § 274(a)(1)(A), the item must be directly related to the taxpayer's business, or, if the item directly precedes or follows a bona fide business discussion, the item must be associated with the active conduct of the taxpayer's business. Section 162(a)(2) allows a deduction for all ordinary and necessary expenses paid or incurred in carrying on any trade or business, including travel expenses in pursuit of a trade or business. But § 274 disallows some deductions that would otherwise qualify under § 162(a)(2). In particular, expenses for entertainment must meet stricter criteria than are imposed under § 162(a)(2) to qualify for deduction. Section 1.274-2(b)(1)(iii) of the Income Tax Regulations provides that where an expenditure might qualify as both a business travel expense and an entertainment expense, it must be construed as an expenditure for entertainment. In this case, the trips taken by Walliser (P) have elements of both business travel and entertainment. It is irrelevant that he took the trips solely to find new business; sightseeing tours, under objective standards, constitute entertainment sufficient to engage § 274(a). Walliser (P) took the trips in the hopes of finding more business. But the "directly related" requirement in § 274 disallows the mere promotion of goodwill in a social setting. There is no firm link between building tours and loan sales at First Federal. Furthermore, the "associated with" requirement of § 274 is not met by Walliser's (P) trip. This element of the test is an exception to the general rule designed to allow deductions for such activities as business dinners that occur in close proximity to substantive business negotiations. A trip cannot be said to relate with temporal proximity to business activities, even where Walliser (P) discussed the possibility of providing loans during the entire trip. The discussions were of a speculative nature only, and not the substantive type of business discussion contemplated by § 274. Decision entered for the Commissioner (D).

EDITOR'S ANALYSIS: The personal element of entertainment expenditures has disturbed the Congress for some time. In an effort to prevent abuse of the entertainment deduction, § 274 was fashioned to force deductions to have a strong link to actual business "deals" of a specific nature, not just discussions seeking business goodwill. The deduction remains available, but the door has been narrowed by § 274.

[For more information on business entertainment expenses, see Casenote Law Outline on Federal Income Taxation, Chapter 7, § I, Expenses Relating to the Production of Income as Opposed to Those Relating to Personal Consumption.]

NOTES:

MOSS v. COMMISSIONER

758 F.2d 211 (7th Cir. 1985).

NATURE OF CASE: Appeal from decision disallowing tax deductions.

FACT SUMMARY: Moss (P) appealed from a Tax Court decision disallowing a tax deduction on his share of his firm's daily business meeting lunch expenses, contending that the business nature of the daily lunch would qualify the lunch expense for necessary business expense treatment.

CONCISE RULE OF LAW: The expenses of daily business meeting lunches among coworkers are not deductible as necessary business expenses, even though the meetings might be necessary from a business perspective.

FACTS: Moss (P) was a partner in a small law firm specializing in trial work. The members of the firm met daily for lunch at Angelo's, a restaurant convenient for their practice. At the meeting, cases were discussed with the head of the firm, and the firm's trial schedule was worked out at these lunch meetings. These meetings were necessary as each member of the firm carried an enormous caseload, requiring the members of the firm to spend most of their day in court. Thus, lunch was the most convenient meeting time, as the courts were then in recess. There was no suggestion that the attorneys dawdled over lunch, or that the restaurant chosen was extravagant. Moss (P) sought to deduct his share of the lunch expenses as a necessary business expense. The Commissioner (D) took the position that the lunch expenses were not deductible. The Tax Court agreed with the Commissioner (D) and disallowed the deductions. From this decision Moss (P) appealed.

ISSUE: Are the expenses of daily business meeting lunches among coworkers deductible as necessary business expenses where the meetings would be considered necessary from a business perspective?

HOLDING AND DECISION: (Posner, J.) Yes. The expenses of daily business meeting lunches among coworkers are not deductible as necessary business expenses, even though the meetings might be necessary from a business perspective. Given the unique nature of the firm's practice there is not much dispute that the meetings themselves were necessary for the smooth functioning of the firm, and that lunch was the most convenient time to hold such meetings. Meals are deductible when they are necessary and ordinary business expenses. There is a natural reluctance to allow deductions for expenses both business and personal in nature and because the meal deduction is allowed, the Commissioner (D) requires that the meal expense be a real business necessity. The considerations involved with business meetings with coworkers are different than where the meetings are among coworkers. In client entertainment situations, the business objective, to be fully achieved, requires the sharing of a meal. In the present situation, the meal was not an organic part of the meeting, even though the meetings were necessary from a business perspective and lunch was the most convenient time for the meeting. In evaluating cases like this, decisions must be based on the frequency of the meetings and the individual degree and circumstance of the luncheon meetings sought to be deducted. In this case, however, the lunches, not being an organic part of the business purpose of the meetings, are not deductible. Affirmed.

EDITOR'S ANALYSIS: The current state of deductibility for expenses as long as a plausible business connection can be demonstrated is particularly unjust to a majority of taxpayers, who cannot take advantage of such deductions by virtue of their employment. Such inequities are most apparent in connection with the deductibility of various entertainment functions, such as tickets to sporting and theatrical events, which involve a significant personal component, and allow a personal subsidy to those in a position to take advantage of business deductions.

[For more information on business expenses, see Casenote Law Outline on Federal Income Taxation, Chapter 7, § I, Expenses Relating to the Production of Income as Opposed to Those Relating to Personal Consumption.]

NOTES:

CHAPTER 17
EDUCATION EXPENSES

QUICK REFERENCE RULES OF LAW

1. **Education Expenses.** Educational expenses are deductible as ordinary and necessary business expenses if the education enhances skills required by the individual in his trade, or if the education meets the express requirements of the individual s employer. (Takahashi v. Commissioner)

   [For more information on educational business expenses, see Casenote Law Outline on Federal Income Taxation, Chapter 7, § I, Expenses Relating to the Production of Income as Opposed to Those Relating to Personal Consumption.]

2. **Education Expenses.** In order for educational expenses to be properly deducted, they must be incurred in maintaining or improving skills of a profession in which the taxpayer is already firmly established. (Wassenaar v. Commissioner)

   [For more information on educational expenses, see Casenote Law Outline on Federal Income Taxation, Chapter 7, § I, Expenses Relating to the Production of Income as Opposed to Those Relating to Personal Consumption.]

3. **Education Expenses.** If the course of study is such that the expense thereof can reasonably be considered ordinary and necessary in carrying on the business of teaching, costs incurred in graduate study are deductible as educational expenses. (Furner v. Commissioner)

   [For more information on educational expenses, see Casenote Law Outline on Federal Income Taxation, Chapter 7, § I, Expenses Relating to the Production of Income as Opposed to Those Relating to Personal Consumption.]

4. **Education Expenses.** (1) All costs of minimum educational requirements for qualification in employment are personal expenditures or constitute an inseparable aggregate of personal and capital expenditures. (2) Capital costs incurred in obtaining a new professional license are amortizable, but educational expenses that qualify an individual for a new trade or business, by virtue of new professional certifications, are not deductible. (Sharon v. Commissioner)

   [For more information on depreciation and amortization/educational expenses, see Casenote Law Outline on Federal Income Taxation, Chapter 5, § I, Depreciation and Depletion and Chapter 7, § I, Expenses Relating to the Production of Income as Opposed to Those Relating to Personal Consumption.]

NOTES

TAKAHASHI v. COMMISSIONER

87 T.C. 126 (1986).

NATURE OF CASE: Suit challenging an IRS denial of a deduction for educational expenses.

FACT SUMMARY: Takahashi (P), a teacher, attended a seminar on cultural diversity in Hawaii in an effort to comply with the discretionary multicultural education requirements of the employing school district.

CONCISE RULE OF LAW: Educational expenses are deductible as ordinary and necessary business expenses if the education enhances skills required by the individual in his trade, or if the education meets the express requirements of the individual's employer.

FACTS: The Takahashis (P) were employed as science teachers in the Los Angeles Unified School District. The California State Education Code required teachers to complete a minimum of two semester units in a course dealing with multiculturalism to receive promotions and raises. In 1981, the Takahashis (P) attended a seminar in Hawaii entitled "The Hawaiian Cultural Transition in a Diverse Society." They attended the seminar on nine of ten days spent in Hawaii. The program lasted from one to six hours a day. The Takahashis (P) spent $2,373 on the trip. They claimed the expenses incurred on the trip as an educational expense. In a deficiency notice, the Commissioner (D) denied the expense in full. The Takahashis (P) filed suit in Tax Court challenging the Commissioner's (D) denial.

ISSUE: Are all educational expenses related to the taxpayer's business or trade deductible?

HOLDING AND DECISION: (Nims, J.) No. Educational expenses are deductible as ordinary and necessary business expenses if the education enhances skills required by the individual in his trade, or if the education meets the express requirements of the individual's employer. In this case, the application of the tax regulations is fairly straightforward. There is no contention in the record that attendance of the Hawaii seminar was required by the school district. Rather, it is argued that the seminar improved teaching skills. But it is a stretch to believe that learning about multiculturalism in Hawaii aided the teaching of science classes in Los Angeles. The Commissioner (D) argues, and the point is well taken, that the burden is upon the taxpayer to show that a reasonable allocation exists between business education expenses on the trip and personal vacation expenditures; no such offering has been made by the Takahashis. Since it is conceded that the trip was not required, and the content of the seminar does not seem rationally linked to the teaching of science, the threshold tests of § 1.162-5(a) of the regulations have not been met. Decision entered for the Commissioner (D).

EDITOR'S ANALYSIS: The 1986 Tax Reform Act expressed great concern over the possibility that teachers could deduct expenses that were primarily personal vacation expenses under the guise of educational expenses. An allocation of costs between personal and business can be made, but the burden is on the taxpayer to prove the allocation is reasonable.

[For more information on educational business expenses, see Casenote Law Outline on Federal Income Taxation, Chapter 7, § I, Expenses Relating to the Production of Income as Opposed to Those Relating to Personal Consumption.]

NOTES:

WASSENAAR v. COMMISSIONER

72 T.C. 1195 (1979).

NATURE OF CASE: Suit seeking to overturn an IRS denial of educational expense deductions.

FACT SUMMARY: An attorney attempted to deduct the cost of obtaining a master's degree in taxation as an employee business expense.

CONCISE RULE OF LAW: In order for educational expenses to be properly deducted, they must be incurred in maintaining or improving skills of a profession in which the taxpayer is already firmly established.

FACTS: Wassenaar (P) graduated from Wayne State University Law School in 1972. He took the bar exam in July 1972 and was notified of a passing score in October 1972. However, he was not formally admitted to the Michigan bar until May 1973. In September 1972, Wassenaar (P) entered the graduate law program in taxation at NYU. He graduated with a master's degree in taxation in May 1973. He incurred expenses of $2,781 completing the master's program. Wassenaar (P) then took his first position as an attorney. On his 1973 taxes, Wassenaar (P) sought to deduct the expenses at NYU as an employee business expense. He received a deficiency notice denying the entire deduction, and he then filed suit in Tax Court.

ISSUE: May the cost of obtaining a master's degree in taxation be deducted as an ordinary and necessary expense incurred in trade or business if the taxpayer has not yet practiced in the profession?

HOLDING AND DECISION: (No judge listed) No. In order for educational expenses to be properly deducted, they must be incurred in maintaining or improving skills of a profession in which the taxpayer is already firmly established. Generally, the cost of learning a trade or profession is not deductible if the taxpayer is learning a new trade or profession. In this case, Wassenaar (P) argued that his education at NYU helped to maintain and improve his skills as an attorney. However, it is a well-established principle that being a member in good standing of a profession is not tantamount to carrying on that profession. Wassenaar (P) had never practiced as an attorney when he enrolled at NYU. In fact, he was not even permitted to practice law as a member of the bar until he was in the process of finishing his coursework at NYU. Thus it cannot be said that he was "improving" his ability to practice a trade or business. His was an ongoing educational endeavor to become a tax law specialist. Accordingly, Wassenaar's (P) educational expenses are not deductible.

EDITOR'S ANALYSIS: The most interesting aspect of this case is the fact that law school graduates invariably assume that a clever characterization of facts is all that is necessary to turn the law on its head. Wassenaar (P) lost because common sense is all that is required to determine that taxpayers cannot maintain and improve skills in a profession in which they don't yet engage. Furthermore, the general approach in the area of tax law has been to narrowly define a trade or business. For example, a pharmacist intern has been held to have a different trade from a licensed pharmacist.

[For more information on educational expenses, see Casenote Law Outline on Federal Income Taxation, Chapter 7, § I, Expenses Relating to the Production of Income as Opposed to Those Relating to Personal Consumption.]

NOTES:

FURNER v. COMMISSIONER

393 F.2d 292 (7th Cir. 1968).

NATURE OF CASE: Appeal of Tax Court decision upholding IRS denial of educational expense deductions.

FACT SUMMARY: Furner (P), a school teacher, left her position and returned to graduate school in order to be more fully versed in relevant subject matter.

CONCISE RULE OF LAW: If the course of study is such that the expense thereof can reasonably be considered ordinary and necessary in carrying on the business of teaching, costs incurred in graduate study are deductible as educational expenses.

FACTS: Furner (P) majored in social studies at a teachers' college, and received a bachelor's degree in 1957. She taught in a Minnesota school, grades seven through twelve, between 1957 and 1960. She primarily taught history, a subject falling under her educational background. However, she felt that her teaching required a greater depth of knowledge than she possessed. Furner (P) arranged to enter a graduate program at Northwestern University as a full-time graduate student during the 1960-61 school year. Because her school system did not readily grant leaves of absence, she resigned in June, 1960. Furner (P) sought to deduct the cost of her graduate education, but she received a deficiency notice that denied the deduction. In her Tax Court suit, the court ruled that she was not carrying on a trade or business of teaching while attending graduate school. She appealed to the court of appeals.

ISSUE: Are costs incurred in graduate study deductible as educational expense?

HOLDING AND DECISION: (Fairchild, J.) Yes. If the course of study is such that the expense thereof can reasonably be considered ordinary and necessary in carrying on the business of teaching, costs incurred in graduate study are deductible as educational expenses. Gaining additional education in a trade or business can be deducted as a business expense where the education maintains or improves on skills necessary to perform in the trade or business. The permissibility of this deduction is not contingent upon whether or not the attainment of additional relevant skills interrupts the carrying on of the trade or business. Certainly, education takes time to accomplish. In this case, the Commissioner (D) focused too much on Furner's (P) year away from teaching. It is becoming usual for teachers to further their professional options by deepening their knowledge in a specific subject. Certainly, Furner (P) might have achieved her graduate degree in part-time studies, but there are factors that make finishing in a single year very attractive. It seems that her enrollment in a graduate program is a normal incident of carrying on the business of teaching. Reversed.

EDITOR'S ANALYSIS: Whether an educational expense deduction will be permitted depends in part on the conventions in the particular trade or business. In this case, the trend in teaching was to return to graduate school if additional skills in a subject were required for advancement and job security. The education must be analyzed in the context of the business or trade in question.

[For more information on educational expenses, see Casenote Law Outline on Federal Income Taxation, Chapter 7, § I, Expenses Relating to the Production of Income as Opposed to Those Relating to Personal Consumption.]

NOTES:

SHARON v. COMMISSIONER

66 T.C. 515 (1976), aff'd 591 F.2d 1273 (9th Cir. 1978).

NATURE OF CASE: Appeal of Tax Court decision upholding an IRS denial of numerous deductions for educational expenses.

FACT SUMMARY: Sharon (P), an attorney, attempted to deduct various bar admission fees and educational expenses incurred in completing licensing requirements.

CONCISE RULE OF LAW: (1) All costs of minimum educational requirements for qualification in employment are personal expenditures or constitute an inseparable aggregate of personal and capital expenditures. (2) Capital costs incurred in obtaining a new professional license are amortizable, but educational expenses that qualify an individual for a new trade or business, by virtue of new professional certifications, are not deductible.

FACTS: Sharon (P) obtained a law degree from Columbia University in 1964. He then took the New York State bar exam, expending $175.20 for bar review courses and materials, and $25 for the bar exam fee. Sharon (P) was admitted to practice in the State of New York on December 22, 1964. He worked there in a law firm until 1967. In 1967, he accepted a position in the Office of Regional Counsel, Internal Revenue Service, and moved to California. Although not required by his employer, Sharon (P) decided to become a member of the California State Bar. He spent $801 on California bar review materials and fees for admission. He also spent $11 in order to be admitted to practice before the U.S. District Court and the U.S. Court of Appeals. Sharon (P) was assessed deficiencies in his tax returns for 1969 and 1970, where he deducted various educational expenses and took amortization deductions on others. The Tax Court generally denied his deductions, with certain minor exceptions, and the Court of Appeals affirmed.

ISSUE: (1) May the costs of obtaining a license to practice law be amortized over expected work life? (2) Are capital costs incurred in obtaining a new professional license amortizable?

HOLDING AND DECISION: (Simpson, J.) (1) No. All costs of minimum educational requirements for qualification in employment are personal expenditures or constitute an inseparable aggregate of personal and capital expenditures. Educational expenses intended to qualify an individual for a trade or business cannot be capitalized. In this case, Sharon (P) attempts to characterize his legal education as an expense incident to obtaining his license to practice law, an amortizable expense. But his clever characterization is not compelling. A law school education provides benefits in numerous ways; he is not limited to the practice of law in New York, and many individuals with law degrees never practice law. The $25 fee for his license could in theory have been amortized as a capital expenditure and deducted in one year due to its minimal value. But the year in question is well passed, and all he may now do is include the remaining portion of that fee in his capital deductions for his California license. The educational amortization is denied. Affirmed. (2) Yes. Capital costs incurred in obtaining a new professional license are amortizable, but educational expenses that qualify an individual for a new trade or business, by virtue of new professional certifications, are not deductible. Where the useful life of a license extends beyond one year, it cannot be deducted as an expense, but rather, it must be treated as a capital expenditure. In this case, the $812 spent by Sharon (P) in acquiring a California license must be divided into two parts: the cost of the review course, an educational expense, and the license fees, a capital expenditure. The bar review course is indeed an educational expense, but if it qualifies Sharon (P) for a new trade, then it is not deductible. The education aided Sharon (P) in receiving his license to practice law in California. Since he could not practice without the license, the bar review course qualified him for a new trade, the practice of law in California. It is not deductible as an educational business expense. The remaining $582 dollars, conferring a professional license, is a capital expenditure with a life expectancy equal to Sharon's (P) projected life expectancy. He may amortize the cost over that period. Affirmed.

DISSENT: (Scott, J.) The license fees should not be amortizable over the life span of Sharon (P). While they are indeed capital expenditures, there is nothing in the record to indicate the useful life of those expenditures. The life span of the asset acquired must be ascertained with fair certainty.

DISSENT: (Irwin, J.) It seems an odd conclusion that an attorney, licensed to practice in New York, has qualified for a new trade or business by virtue of being licensed in California. The bar exam ought to be treated as part of the cost of acquiring the license to practice in California.

EDITOR'S ANALYSIS: This case provides an excellent example of the difficulty in characterizing expended funds as either capital investments or expenses. The primary factor that determines the characterization is the useful life of the asset.

[For more information on depreciation and amortization/educational expenses, see Casenote Law Outline on Federal Income Taxation, Chapter 5, § I, Depreciation and Depletion and Chapter 7, § I, Expenses Relating to the Production of Income as Opposed to Those Relating to Personal Consumption.]

NOTES:

CHAPTER 18
MOVING EXPENSES, CHILD CARE, LEGAL EXPENSES, CLOTHING

QUICK REFERENCE RULES OF LAW

1. **Child Care Expenses.** Any claimed child care expenditure must be justified as both allowing the taxpayer to work and providing for the "care" of the taxpayer's child. (Zoltan v. Commissioner)

   [For more information on child care deductions, see Casenote Law Outline on Federal Income Taxation, Chapter 7, § II, Deductions for Personal Outlays.]

2. **Clothing Expenses.** Clothing cost is deductible as a business expense only if the clothing is specifically required as a condition of employment, it is not adaptable to general usage as ordinary clothing, and it is not so worn. (Pevsner v. Commissioner)

   [For more information on prerequisites to deductibility, see Casenote Law Outline on Federal Income Taxation, Chapter 7, § I, Expenses Relating to the Production of Income as Opposed to Those

Notes

ZOLTAN v. COMMISSIONER

79 T.C. 490 (1982).

NATURE OF CASE: Suit challenging an IRS denial of deductions claimed as child care expenses.

FACT SUMMARY: Zoltan (P) incurred expenses sending her son to a summer camp and on a school trip, and she then sought to deduct them as child care expenses.

CONCISE RULE OF LAW: Any claimed child care expenditure must be justified as both allowing the taxpayer to work and providing for the "care" of the taxpayer's child.

FACTS: Zoltan (P) worked as an accountant, and her job kept her away from home roughly fifty hours a week. Her son, Paul, was eleven years old in 1977. In 1977, $1,180 was paid to Camp Adanac, a summer camp where Paul spent eight weeks. The camp provided food, lodging, supervision, and instruction in various activities such as swimming. In 1978, $116 was paid by Zoltan (P) to cover the cost of a school trip taken by Paul during his Easter vacation. Zoltan (P) deducted these amounts on her taxes as child care expenses. The Commissioner (D) denied the deductions, and Zoltan (P) filed suit in Tax Court, challenging the ruling.

ISSUE: Must any claimed child care expenditure be justified as both permitting the taxpayer to work and providing for the "care" of the taxpayer's child?

HOLDING AND DECISION: (Sterrett, J.) Yes. Any claimed child care expenditure must be justified as both allowing the taxpayer to work and providing for the "care" of the taxpayer's child. In this case, the first element is easily satisfied; the expenses permitted Zoltan (P) to meet her work obligations. The more difficult issue is whether the expenses cover "care" of the child. To qualify as expenses for child care, the primary purpose of the care must be to assure the well-being and protection of the child. Here, the summer camp clearly qualifies as an expense to assure the well-being and protection of Paul. The camp was supervised by adults at all times, and Paul was given safe lodging. The school trip also qualifies as an expense to assure the well-being and protection of Paul. The school trip was also supervised by adults. In both instances, Paul was watched during vacation periods where, left to his own devices, he could have placed himself in harm's way. The deductions are appropriate; the Commissioner's (D) denial is overruled.

EDITOR'S ANALYSIS: Subsequent to this case, § 21 has been amended in 1987 to disqualify overnight camp expenses as employment related. The case may be of reduced precedential value now. Compare Perry v. Commissioner, 92 T.C. 470 (1989), where the cost of plane tickets for children being sent to visit their grandparents was characterized by the Tax Court as transportation expenses, not child care.

[For more information on child care deductions, see Casenote Law Outline on Federal Income Taxation, Chapter 7, § II, Deductions for Personal Outlays.]

NOTES:

PEVSNER v. COMMISSIONER
628 F.2d 467 (5th Cir. 1980).

NATURE OF CASE: Appeal from decision upholding a business expense deduction.

FACT SUMMARY: Pevsner (P) contended that because clothing she was required to purchase and wear in her employment was not consistent with her personal lifestyle, she could deduct their cost as a business expense.

CONCISE RULE OF LAW: Clothing cost is deductible as a business expense only if the clothing is specifically required as a condition of employment, it is not adaptable to general usage as ordinary clothing, and it is not so worn.

FACTS: Pevsner (P) was employed as the manager of the Sakowitz Yves St. Laurent Rive Gauche Boutique, which sold only women's clothes designed by Yves St. Laurent, a famous designer. The clothing was highly fashionable and expensively priced. Pevsner (P) was required as a condition of her employment to wear Yves St. Laurent clothes while working. She purchased $1,381.91 worth of the clothes and wore them exclusively at work. At home she lived a very simple life and the clothes would not be consistent with this lifestyle. She deducted the cost of clothes as a business expense, yet the IRS (D) disallowed the deduction contending she could have worn the clothes away from work and her choice not to was irrelevant to the deductibility of the clothes. The Tax Court allowed the deduction, and the IRS (D) appealed.

ISSUE: Is clothing cost a deductible business expense only if the clothing is specifically required as a condition of employment, it is not adaptable to general usage as ordinary clothing, and it is not so worn?

HOLDING AND DECISION: (Johnson, J.) Yes. Clothing cost is deductible as a business expense only if the clothing is specifically required as a condition of employment, it is not adaptable to general use as ordinary clothing, and it is not so worn. In this case, the clothing was clearly a condition of employment. However, it was only by choice that Pevsner (P) failed to wear the clothing away from work. This element must be determined by an objective test. If a deduction were allowed on the subjective attitude of the taxpayer, no workable guidelines for the deduction could be developed. Therefore, because the clothing was adaptable to ordinary use the deduction cannot be allowed. Reversed.

EDITOR'S ANALYSIS: The use of this objective test in determining whether clothing is deductible under §§ 162 and 262 avoids an unfair application of the deduction. The subjective test would allow similarly situated taxpayers to be treated differently according to their lifestyle and socio-economic level. The objective test allows the greatest level of fairness to the greatest number of taxpayers.

[For more information on prerequisites to deductibility, see Casenote Law Outline on Federal Income Taxation, Chapter 7, § I, Expenses Relating to the Production of Income as Opposed to Those Relating to Personal Consumption.]

NOTES:

CHAPTER 19
HOBBY LOSSES

QUICK REFERENCE RULES OF LAW

1. **Deductions Allowable under Section 183.** Deductible losses under § 183 of the Internal Revenue Code are allowed if the taxpayer entered into the activity with the actual and honest objective of making a profit. (Dreicer v. Commissioner)

   [For more information on deductibility of expenses, see Casenote Law Outline on Federal Income Taxation, Chapter 7, § I, Expenses Relating to the Production of Income as Opposed to Those Relating to Personal Consumption.]

2. **Deductions Allowable under Section 183.** In determining whether an activity is engaged in for profit, objective facts regarding the manner, success, and history of the taxpayer's efforts are given greater weight than the taxpayer's stated intent. (Remuzzi v. Commissioner)

   [For more information on deductibility of expenses, see Casenote Law Outline on Federal Income Taxation, Chapter 7, § I, Expenses Relating to the Production of Income as Opposed to Those Relating to Personal Consumption.]

Notes

DREICER v. COMMISSIONER

78 T.C. 642 (1982).

NATURE OF CASE: Remand from court of appeals reversal of decision upholding notice of deficiency.

FACT SUMMARY: Dreicer (P) claimed deductible losses for expenses related to his alleged profession as a writer.

CONCISE RULE OF LAW: Deductible losses under § 183 of the Internal Revenue Code are allowed if the taxpayer entered into the activity with the actual and honest objective of making a profit.

FACTS: Dreicer (P), an independently wealthy man, spent many years traveling around the world in fine style, ostensibly for the purpose of writing a travel book. His manuscript was rejected by the two publishing companies he submitted it to. Dreicer (P) claimed deductible losses of approximately $50,000 in 1972 and 1973 for travel expenses. The Commissioner (D) disallowed the deductions on the ground that the expenses arose from activities not pursued for profit. The Tax Court upheld the notice of deficiency, holding that Dreicer (P) had no reasonable expectation of profits from his writings. The court of appeals reversed and remanded, ruling that the Tax Court had not used the proper legal standard.

ISSUE: Are deductible losses under § 183 of the Internal Revenue Code allowed if the taxpayer entered into the activity with the actual and honest objective of making a profit?

HOLDING AND DECISION: (Simpson, J.) Yes. Deductible losses under § 183 of the Internal Revenue Code are allowed if the taxpayer entered into the activity with the actual and honest objective of making a profit. Deductions for business expenses under § 183 must be allowed where the taxpayer has an honest objective of profits even though there may be no reasonable expectation of profits. Thus, the taxpayer's motive is the ultimate question. This motive must be determined by a careful analysis of all the surrounding objective facts. The taxpayer's statement of intent should be only one of the relevant factors. In the present case, Dreicer (P) sustained large losses for many years. Thus, the objective facts of the case show that there was no realistic possibility that he could ever earn sufficient income to offset the losses. The expenses arose from activities that were not conducted in a businesslike manner calculated to earn a profit. Accordingly, the prior decision affirming the Commissioner (D) is re-entered.

EDITOR'S ANALYSIS: Dreicer (P) wanted to be treated in the same manner as an inventor or wildcat driller would be treated; those examples are mentioned in the applicable regulations to § 183. These types of endeavors are continued in the face of large losses in the hope of a giant payoff. Ultimately, the Tax Court simply did not believe that Dreicer's (P) travels were actually undertaken to make money.

[For more information on deductibility of expenses, see Casenote Law Outline on Federal Income Taxation, Chapter 7, § I, Expenses Relating to the Production of Income as Opposed to Those Relating to Personal Consumption.]

NOTES:

REMUZZI v. COMMISSIONER

T.C. Memo 1988-8 ___.

NATURE OF CASE: Appeal from disallowance of deductions.

FACT SUMMARY: Remuzzi (P), a surgeon, claimed losses from operating a farm where his family lived.

CONCISE RULE OF LAW: In determining whether an activity is engaged in for profit, objective facts regarding the manner, success, and history of the taxpayer's efforts are given greater weight than the taxpayer's stated intent.

FACTS: Remuzzi (P), a surgeon, bought a large piece of property in 1978. The property, Farleigh Farm, contained old farm buildings but had not been operated as a farm for ten years. Remuzzi (P) made an agreement with Payne, one of his patients, whereby Payne was to raise cattle on the farm as a tenant. However, shortly thereafter, Payne was not able to work and Remuzzi (P) made some efforts to operate Farleigh Farm using his family and hired help. Remuzzi (P) reported revenues and expenses from the farm from 1978 to 1982. The revenues were extremely minimal while the losses were significant. The Commissioner (D) disallowed much of the claimed losses on the basis that Farleigh Farm was not operated for profit.

ISSUE: Are objective facts regarding the manner, success, and history of the taxpayer's efforts given greater weight than the taxpayer's stated intent when determining whether an activity is engaged in for profit?

HOLDING AND DECISION: (Korner, J.) Yes. In determining whether an activity is engaged in for profit, objective facts regarding the manner, success, and history of the taxpayer's efforts are given greater weight than the taxpayer's stated intent. Section 183 of the Internal Revenue Code allows for deductible expenses if an activity is engaged in for profit. Whether a taxpayer's objective is bona fide is a question of fact to be determined from all of the facts and circumstances and not just from the taxpayer's stated intent. Section 183's regulations list nine factors that should be taken into account: (1) the manner in which the taxpayer conducts the activity; (2) the expertise of the taxpayer; (3) the time and effort expended; (4) the expectation of asset appreciation; (5) the success of similar operations; (6) the history of the taxpayer; (7) amount of profits; (8) the financial status of the taxpayer; and (9) the personal pleasure gained by the taxpayer. These factors create an objective standard for making the determination. In the instant case the most important factors are that Remuzzi (P) had substantial income from his primary profession and the claimed losses reduced his tax burden. Also, there is no evidence that Remuzzi (P) treated Farleigh Farm as a business by trying to reduce expenses and maximize revenues. Remuzzi (P) had no expertise and spent little time operating the farm. Finally, it is evident that Remuzzi (P) and his family moved to the farm for personal enjoyment and pleasure. Accordingly, Remuzzi (P) failed to prove that Farleigh Farm was engaged in for profit.

EDITOR'S ANALYSIS: Another key factor in this case was that Farleigh Farm suffered such large and consistent losses. The case also dealt with Remuzzi's (P) claim that an unpaid loan to Payne was a bad business debt. The Tax Court found that since the farm was not a business, a bad debt related to the farm could not be a bad business debt.

[For more information on deductibility of expenses, see Casenote Law Outline on Federal Income Taxation, Chapter 7, § I, Expenses Relating to the Production of Income as Opposed to Those Relating to Personal Consumption.]

NOTES:

CHAPTER 20
HOME OFFICES, VACATION HOMES AND OTHER DUAL USE PROPERTY

QUICK REFERENCE RULES OF LAW

1. **Other Dual Use Property.** A comparative analysis of the functions performed is necessary to determine whether a home office qualifies as a taxpayer's principal place of business. (Soliman v. Commissioner)

   [For more information on deductibility of expenses, see Casenote Law Outline on Federal Income Taxation, Chapter 7, § II, Deductions for Personal Outlays.]

Notes

SOLIMAN v. COMMISSIONER

_U.S._, 113 S. Ct. 701 (1993).

NATURE OF CASE: Appeal from disallowance of home office deductions.

FACT SUMMARY: Soliman (P), an anesthesiologist, claimed deductions for his home office, where he handled his scheduling and paperwork.

CONCISE RULE OF LAW: A comparative analysis of the functions performed is necessary to determine whether a home office qualifies as a taxpayer's principal place of business.

FACTS: Soliman (P) practiced as an anesthesiologist in Maryland and Virginia. He spent thirty to thirty-five hours a week with patients at hospitals that did not provide him with an office. Soliman (P) used a spare bedroom at his home as an office. He did not meet patients there, but spent two to three hours a day maintaining his records, preparing for treatments, and generally performing necessary office work. Soliman (P) claimed deductions for this home office on his tax return. The Commissioner (D) disallowed the deductions based upon his determination that the home office was not Soliman's (P) principal place of business. Soliman (P) prevailed on his petition to Tax Court and again at the circuit court level. The Commissioner (D) appealed.

ISSUE: Is a comparative analysis of the functions performed necessary to determine whether a home office qualifies as a taxpayer's principal place of business?

HOLDING AND DECISION: (Kennedy, J.) Yes. A comparative analysis of the functions performed is necessary to determine whether a home office qualifies as a taxpayer's principal place of business. Section 280(a) of the Internal Revenue Code was adopted as part of the Tax Reform Act of 1976. Previously, expenses attributable to home offices were deductible where they were "appropriate and helpful" to the business. The new statute provides a narrower scope, allowing deductions only where the home office is the "principal place of business." Although this term is not defined, the common meaning of "principal" suggests that a comparison of business locations must be undertaken. Ultimately, the determination is dependent on the particular facts and circumstances of each case. However, the two primary considerations are the relative importance of the activities performed at each business location and the time spent there. While visits by clients, customers, or patients are not a required characteristic of the principal place of business, they are a relevant factor. In the present case, Soliman's (P) primary job was to treat patients at hospitals; it was the essence of his professional service. Although careful planning and study at home were necessary, they were less important and took less time than the actual treatment. Accordingly, Soliman (P) is not entitled to the home office deductions. Reversed.

EDITOR'S ANALYSIS: The court of appeals decision reversed by this opinion had placed the most weight on the facts that Soliman's (P) home activities were necessary and other office space was unavailable. This case makes it much more difficult for taxpayers to claim home office deductions. Sales people who spend most of their time meeting clients also will have a difficult time showing that their home offices are principal places of business.

[For more information on deductibility of expenses, see Casenote Law Outline on Federal Income Taxation, Chapter 7, § II, Deductions for Personal Outlays.]

NOTES:

Notes

CHAPTER 21
THE INTEREST DEDUCTION

QUICK REFERENCE RULES OF LAW

1. **Timing Issues and Limitations.** Interest deductions are allowed only if the interest is actually paid in the taxable year. (Battelstein v. Commissioner)

    [For more information on deductibility of expenses, see Casenote Law Outline on Federal Income Taxation, Chapter 7, § I, Expenses Relating to the Production of Income as Opposed to Those Relating to Personal Consumption.]

Notes

BATTELSTEIN v. COMMISSIONER

631 F.2d 1182 (5th Cir. 1980).

NATURE OF CASE: Appeal from decision overruling a notice of deficiency.

FACT SUMMARY: Battelstein (P) claimed interest deductions from a real estate loan although the lender actually returned the amount of interest paid and deferred the obligation.

CONCISE RULE OF LAW: Interest deductions are allowed only if the interest is actually paid in the taxable year.

FACTS: Battelstein (P), a land developer, borrowed $3 million to purchase Sharpstown from Gibraltar. Gibraltar also agreed to make future advances to Battelstein (P) of the interest costs on the loan as they came due. Thus, each quarter Battelstein (P) paid the amount of interest due and Gibraltar then sent back a check for the same amount. Battelstein (P) claimed interest deductions under Internal Revenue Code § 163. The Commissioner (D) found that Battelstein (P) had not actually paid interest in the relevant taxable year and disallowed the deduction. On appeal, the district court ruled for Battelstein (P). The Commissioner (D) appealed.

ISSUE: Are interest deductions allowed only if the interest is actually paid in the taxable year?

HOLDING AND DECISION: (Johnson, J.) Yes. Interest deductions are allowed only if the interest is actually paid in the taxable year. Section 163 of the Internal Revenue Code allows for interest deductions for the current payment of interest in cash or its equivalent. In tax cases it is appropriate to look through the form in which the taxpayer has cloaked a transaction and find the substance of the transaction. In the present case, the future advance loans made by Gibraltar to Battelstein (P) were plainly for no purpose other than to finance Battelstein's (P) current interest obligations. Thus, the check exchanges did not truly result in the payment of interest by Battelstein (P), but were merely deferments of interest obligations. Reversed.

DISSENT: (Politz, J.) To determine whether there is a dual loan transaction sham, the court should look to see if there are valid and legitimate reasons for the second loan, whether the proceeds of the second loan are commingled with the taxpayer's other funds, whether the taxpayer has available funds to pay the interest, and whether the borrower loses control of the second loan. Analysis of these factors shows that the subsequent loans to Battelstein (P) were legitimate.

EDITOR'S ANALYSIS: The case of Wilkerson v. Commissioner, 655 F.2d 980 (9th Cir. 1981), reached the same conclusion as the majority decision above. In that case, the loan agreement provided that the financing fee would be paid from segregated loan proceeds unless the borrower paid it. The Internal Revenue Service, through IR-83-93, announced that it would follow these decisions.

[For more information on deductibility of expenses, see Casenote Law Outline on Federal Income Taxation, Chapter 7, § I, Expenses Relating to the Production of Income as Opposed to Those Relating to Personal Consumption.]

NOTES:

Notes

CHAPTER 23
CASUALTY LOSSES

QUICK REFERENCE RULES OF LAW

1. **Insurance Coverage.** Under certain circumstances, taxpayers are not required to eliminate all possible noncasualty causes of a loss in order to claim a § 165 deduction. (Popa v. Commissioner)

[For more information on casualty losses, see Casenote Law Outline on Federal Income Taxation, Chapter 4, § IV, Recognition of Gains and Losses.]

***There are no cases in Chapter 22.**

Notes

POPA v. COMMISSIONER

73 T.C. 130 (1979).

NATURE OF CASE: Appeal from Commissioner's denial of a § 165 casualty loss.

FACT SUMMARY: Popa (P), an executive in Vietnam, lost his possessions when the government collapsed and Americans were ordered evacuated.

CONCISE RULE OF LAW: Under certain circumstances, taxpayers are not required to eliminate all possible noncasualty causes of a loss in order to claim a § 165 deduction.

FACTS: Popa (P) was a vice president with Transworld Services Corp. residing in Saigon, Vietnam in 1975. Days after Popa (P) took a business trip to Thailand, the South Vietnamese government collapsed and Americans were evacuated from the country. Popa (P) was unable to return for his possessions at his home in Saigon. Popa (P) claimed a casualty loss deduction pursuant to § 165(c)(3) of the Internal Revenue Code for the loss of his possessions. The Commissioner (D) disallowed the deduction based on the fact that Popa (P) could not prove how the possessions were lost.

ISSUE: Are taxpayers required to eliminate all possible noncasualty causes of a loss to qualify for a § 165 deduction?

HOLDING AND DECISION: (Sterrett, J.) No. Under certain circumstances, taxpayers are not required to eliminate all possible noncasualty causes of a loss in order to claim a § 165 deduction. Section 165(c)(3) of the Internal Revenue Code allows for a deduction under the category of "other casualty" losses. This section was designed to address sudden, cataclysmic, and devastating losses. The principle of ejusdem generis provides that unexpected, accidental forces exerted against property which are similar to the enumerated causes in § 165 also qualify for casualty losses. In unusual circumstances such as the one faced by Popa (P), it is not fair or reasonable to require the taxpayer to eliminate all possible noncasualty causes of the loss. It is clear that the only conceivable circumstance that would deny Popa (P) a casualty loss would be if his property were confiscated under the authority of some hastily enacted local law. All of the other possibilities would entitle him to the deduction. Accordingly, the most reasonable conclusion is that Popa (P) suffered a qualifying casualty loss.

DISSENT: (Fay, J.) The taxpayer has the burden of proof for alleged casualty losses. Popa (P) cannot prove the cause of his loss and has failed to meet the burden of proof. The taxpayer must bear the misfortune when there is an impossibility of proving the essential facts.

EDITOR'S ANALYSIS: Although the dissent's position is harsh, it is well supported by the Supreme Court's decision in Burnet v. Houston, 283 U.S. 223 (1931). In Burnet, the taxpayer contended that it was impossible for him to prove his 1913 basis for stock that became worthless in 1920. The Court held that, therefore, his claim was unenforceable. The majority decision in Popa does not persuasively distinguish Popa from Burnet. However, it appears that the majority was simply ruling that there was an overwhelming likelihood that Popa's (P) possessions were stolen or destroyed in the war, given what evidence was available.

[For more information on casualty losses, see Casenote Law Outline on Federal Income Taxation, Chapter 4, § IV, Recognition of Gains and Losses.]

NOTES:

Notes

CHAPTER 24
MEDICAL EXPENSES

QUICK REFERENCE RULES OF LAW

1. **Medical Expenses.** Food and lodging expenses incurred while transporting a patient to the place of medication are deductible. (Montgomery v. Commissioner)

[For more information on deductibility of expenses, see Casenote Law Outline on Federal Income Taxation, Chapter 7, § II, Deductions for Personal Outlays.]

NOTES

MONTGOMERY v. COMMISSIONER

428 F.2d 243 (6th Cir. 1970).

NATURE OF CASE: Appeal from disallowance of medical expense deductions.

FACT SUMMARY: Montgomery (P) claimed that food and lodging expenses incurred while driving to the Mayo Clinic were deductible medical expenses.

CONCISE RULE OF LAW: Food and lodging expenses incurred while transporting a patient to the place of medication are deductible.

FACTS: Montgomery (P) and his wife made three round trips from their home in Kentucky to the Mayo Clinic in Minnesota for required medical treatment. During these trips, Montgomery (P) incurred a total expense for meals and lodging of $162. Montgomery (P) deducted this amount pursuant to § 213 of the Internal Revenue Code as medical expenses. The Commissioner (D) disallowed the deductions but the Tax Court ruled for Montgomery (P). The Commissioner (D) appealed.

ISSUE: Are food and lodging expenses incurred while transporting a patient to the place of medication deductible?

HOLDING AND DECISION: (Celebrezze, J.) Yes. Food and lodging expenses incurred while transporting a patient to the place of medication are deductible. Under the Internal Revenue Code of 1939, all food and lodging expenses of a patient on the way to, and at, the place of medication were deductible. These liberal provisions led to significant abuses as taxpayers would travel on doctors' orders to resort areas and deduct all of their expenses. The revised Internal Revenue Code of 1954 sought to eliminate resort area medication abuse. Thus, Congress eliminated the deductibility of food and lodging expenses at the actual place of medication but kept the transportation costs. The legislative history of the revised statute shows that Congress aimed to curb only the resort abuses and sought to continue the deductibility of traveling and transportation costs to the place of medication. Therefore, Montgomery's (P) expenses should have been allowed as proper medical expense deductions under § 213. Affirmed.

EDITOR'S ANALYSIS: Revenue Ruling 78-266 deals with the cost of child care while parents seek medical treatment. It follows court decisions that have held that these expenses are not deductible. Only expenditures that are directly for medical expenses qualify.

[For more information on deductibility of expenses, see Casenote Law Outline on Federal Income Taxation, Chapter 7, § II, Deductions for Personal Outlays.]

NOTES:

Notes

CHAPTER 25
CHARITABLE DEDUCTIONS

QUICK REFERENCE RULES OF LAW

1. **Bargain Sale to Charity.** Taxpayers may claim deductions for charitable contributions only if the money goes directly to the organization or to trusts or foundations. (Davis v. United States)

   [For more information on deductibility of expenses, see Casenote Law Outline on Federal Income Taxation, Chapter 7, § II, Deductions for Personal Outlays.]

Notes

DAVIS v. UNITED STATES

495 U.S. 472 (1990).

NATURE OF CASE: Appeal of disallowance of deductions for charitable contributions.

FACT SUMMARY: Davis (P) provided his sons with funds that allowed the young men to work as missionaries for the Mormon Church and then sought to claim a charitable contribution deduction.

CONCISE RULE OF LAW: Taxpayers may claim deductions for charitable contributions only if the money goes directly to the organization or to trusts or foundations.

FACTS: Davis (P) and his sons, Benjamin and Cecil, belonged to the Church of Jesus Christ of Latter-day Saints. The Mormon Church operates a worldwide missionary program, mostly of young men. The individual missionary's parents generally provide the necessary funds to support their children during the period of service. Missionaries receive some supervision over their use of funds but are not required to obtain advance approval of their expenditures. When Benjamin and Cecil were called as missionaries, Davis (P) provided a total of $6,000 to his sons for their expenses while on their missions. Davis (P) then claimed this money as a deductible charitable contribution on his tax return. The IRS (D) disallowed the deductions and Davis (P) filed suit. His summary judgment motion failed in both the district court and the court of appeals. The Supreme Court granted certiorari.

ISSUE: May taxpayers claim deductions for charitable contributions for all money given that benefits the organization?

HOLDING AND DECISION: (O'Connor, J.) No. Taxpayers may claim deductions for charitable contributions only if the money goes directly to the organization or to trusts or foundations. Section 170 of the Internal Revenue Code provides that taxpayers may claim a deduction for charitable contribution only if the contribution is made "to or for the use of" a qualified organization. Davis (P) contended that the funds given to his sons were "for the use of" the Church. This term could support many meanings based on the plain language of the statute. However, the legislative history shows that Congress had a specific meaning in mind. The original version of § 170 required that the contribution be given directly to the organization. Representatives of charitable foundations then requested an amendment making gifts to trust companies deductible even though the trustee held legal title to the funds. Thus, the "for the use of" language was added to allow for contributions to trusts and foundations. The IRS (D) has subsequently adopted regulations that adopt this approach to the section. In the present case, there is no suggestion that Davis's (P) funds were used for improper purposes or for tax evasion. Still, the funds were not transferred to the Church or in trust for the Church. The money was kept in Benjamin and Cecil's personal accounts and they had no legal obligation to spend the money for the Church. Accordingly, the deductions must be disallowed and the court of appeals affirmed.

EDITOR'S ANALYSIS: The court also rejected Davis's (P) contention that the money could be considered unreimbursed expenditures made incident to the rendition of services. The court found that taxpayers may deduct only those expenditures incurred in connection with the taxpayer's own contributions of service. This holding is consistent with Treasury Regulation § 1.170.A-1(g).

[For more information on deductibility of expenses, see Casenote Law Outline on Federal Income Taxation, Chapter 7, § II, Deductions for Personal Outlays.]

NOTES:

Notes

CHAPTER 26
LIMITATIONS ON DEDUCTIONS

QUICK REFERENCE RULES OF LAW

1. **Transactions between Related Fields.** Congress intended, because of the near economic identity of the parties, to disallow sales between members of certain designated groups. (McWilliams v. Commissioner)

   [For more information on transactions involving related parties, see Casenote Law Outline on Federal Income Taxation, Chapter 4, § IV, Recognition of Gains and Losses.]

2. **Transactions between Related Fields.** Section 267 provides for an absolute ban on deductions for losses on transactions involving family members. (Miller v. Commissioner)

   [For more information on capital gains, see Casenote Law Outline on Federal Income Taxation, Chapter 4, § V, Capital Gains and Losses.]

Notes

McWILLIAMS v. COMMISSIONER

331 U.S. 694 (1947).

NATURE OF CASE: Appeal from circuit court's affirmance of Commissioner's (D) decision to deny deduction for loss incurred on the sale of stock.

FACT SUMMARY: Mr. McWilliams (P) sold shares of stock from his and his wife's estate and purchased the same number of shares of the same stock for the estate of the other spouse.

CONCISE RULE OF LAW: Congress intended, because of the near economic identity of the parties, to disallow sales between members of certain designated groups.

FACTS: Mr. McWilliams (P) managed his and his wife's independent estates. McWilliams (P) often sold shares from one estate or the other and then purchased the same number of shares of the same stock for the estate of the other spouse. Sales and purchases were made through the stock exchange. McWilliams (P) claimed capital deductions on losses sustained through these transactions. The Commissioner (D) disallowed them based on § 267(a)(1). McWilliams (P) appealed claiming that § 267(a)(1) only applies to intrafamily transfers and not to legitimate sales and purchases through the exchange. The court of appeals affirmed and McWilliams (P) appealed.

ISSUE: Should § 267(a)(1) apply to situations where the prohibited transaction involves a third party?

HOLDING AND DECISION: (Vinson, C.J.) Yes. It is true that these were bona fide sales made through a public market. However, the end result is exactly the same as that which Congress sought to prohibit under 267(a)(1). Where a controlled group such as a family unit exists, there is a near-identity of economic interest. Transfers of property between members of these groups do not yield real economic losses. They are mere paper transactions. The loss to one is offset by a corresponding gain by the other. The introduction of a third party into the transaction does not change this result. Therefore, the transaction fits within the evil Congress sought to eliminate. There would be no useful purpose served in limiting 267(a)(1) in this manner. The decision of the Commissioner (D) is affirmed.

EDITOR'S ANALYSIS: In Merritt v. Commissioner, 400 F.2d 417 (5th Cir. 1968), the court held that § 267 precluded a loss deduction where stock owned by taxpayer was involuntarily sold on a distress sale and was purchased by the wife. Section 267 reaches many other types of related taxpayers. The statute and regulations thereunder should be consulted to determine which entities are considered "related." However, the facts of any given transaction may be determinative as to whether gains or loss will be allowed or allocated by the Commissioner.

[For more information on transactions involving related parties, see Casenote Law Outline on Federal Income Taxation, Chapter 4, § IV, Recognition of Gains and Losses.]

NOTES:

MILLER v. COMMISSIONER

75 T.C. 182 (1980).

NATURE OF CASE: Appeal from disallowance of deductions for capital losses.

FACT SUMMARY: David Miller (P) was forced to sell his shares of the business he shared with his brother when their relationship became strained.

CONCISE RULE OF LAW: Section 267 provides for an absolute ban on deductions for losses on transactions involving family members.

FACTS: Charles Miller, the sole shareholder in Charles Miller, Inc., died and left his shares and some real estate to his sons, David (P) and Marvin. Many years later, a serious dispute arose between David (P) and Marvin and arbitrators were retained to resolve the matter. The brothers refused to talk to each other and still do not. The arbitrators decided that David (P) must sell his share of the business and real estate to Marvin, which he reluctantly did. David (P) then claimed a long-term capital loss on his tax return from the sale. The Commissioner (D) disallowed the deduction on the basis of § 267. David (P) filed a petition in Tax Court.

ISSUE: Does § 267 allow deductions for losses on transactions involving family members under certain circumstances?

HOLDING AND DECISION: (Dawson, J.) No. Section 267 provides for an absolute ban on deductions for losses on transactions involving family members. Section 267 of the Internal Revenue Code prohibits deductions for losses sustained from sales or exchanges of property between related parties. The family relationship described in § 267(c)(4) does not require a current relationship. Congress did not intend for courts to examine the intimate relationships between people. The provision was intended to provide an absolute ban without regard to the individual circumstances of some cases. Moreover, the provision does not provide for a rebuttable presumption that could be defeated by a showing of hostility between the parties or the involuntariness of the transaction. In the present case, there is no question that David (P) and Marvin were the natural children of the same parents. Therefore, they are brothers within the meaning of § 267, and the transaction at issue cannot be the basis for a capital loss deduction under any circumstances. The Commissioner (D) is affirmed.

EDITOR'S ANALYSIS: The court noted that § 267 might be seemingly unfair in certain cases but that it was fair to the great majority of taxpayers. Certainly, the court was correct in pointing out the difficulty that courts would have in looking behind the sale at the exact relationship among family members at the time of sales. The bright line test established by this statute makes enforcement easy.

[For more information on capital gains, see Casenote Law Outline on Federal Income Taxation, Chapter 4, § V, Capital Gains and Losses.]

NOTES:

CHAPTER 27
CASH METHOD ACCOUNTING

QUICK REFERENCE RULES OF LAW

1. **Deductions under the Cash Method.** If a promise to pay of a solvent obligor is unconditional and assignable, not subject to set-offs, and is of a kind that is frequently transferred to lenders or investors at a discount not substantially greater than the generally prevailing premium for the use of money, such promise is the equivalent of cash and taxable in like manner as cash had cash been received by the taxpayer rather than the obligation. (Cowden v. Commissioner)

   [For more information on the cash equivalency doctrine, see Casenote Law Outline on Federal Income Taxation, Chapter 8, § II, Tax Accounting Methods.]

2. **Deductions under the Cash Method.** Taxpayers may shift income recognition of a purchase-sale contract by deferred payment through an escrow arrangement if it is part of a bona fide arm's length agreement and the seller receives no present beneficial interest from the funds. (Reed v. Commissioner)

   [For more information on cash method accounting, see Casenote Law Outline on Federal Income Taxation, Chapter 8, § II, Tax Accounting Methods.]

3. **Deductions under the Cash Method.** Expenditures are treated as capital expenses only if they create an asset having a useful life in excess of one year. (Zaninovich v. Commissioner)

   [For more information on cash method accounting, see Casenote Law Outline on Federal Income Taxation Chapter 8, § II, Tax Accounting Methods.]

4. **Deductions under the Cash Method.** Prepaid items are deductible only if there is actual payment for a substantial business reason and prepayment does not create a material distortion of the taxpayer's income in the year of prepayment. (Grynberg v. Commissioner)

   [For more information on cash method accounting, see Casenote Law Outline on Federal Income Taxation, Chapter 8, § II, Tax Accounting Methods.]

Notes

COWDEN v. COMMISSIONER

289 F.2d 20 (5th Cir. 1961).

NATURE OF CASE: Appeal from determination of tax liability.

FACT SUMMARY: Cowden (P), who made an oil, gas, and mineral lease to Stanolind, contracted to receive "advance royalties" over a period of time from Stanolind, such royalties to be paid unconditionally and in any event.

CONCISE RULE OF LAW: If a promise to pay of a solvent obligor is unconditional and assignable, not subject to set-offs, and is of a kind that is frequently transferred to lenders or investors at a discount not substantially greater than the generally prevailing premium for the use of money, such promise is the equivalent of cash and taxable in like manner as cash had cash been received by the taxpayer rather than the obligation.

FACTS: Cowden (P), his wife (P), and children (P) made an oil, gas, and mineral lease to Stanolind Oil and Gas Company upon certain lands in Texas. By supplemental agreements, Stanolind agreed in 1951 to pay advance royalties totaling $511,192.50. The sum of $10,223.85 was payable upon execution of the instruments, $250,484.31 was due between January 5 and 10, 1952, and $250,484.34 was due between January 5 and 10, 1953. The agreement recited that payment would be made "in any event," whether or not Stanolind even continued to have its leasehold interest. Cowden (P), in 1952, assigned Stanolind's 1953 obligation to the bank of which he was president, discounted by 4% per each party. The Commissioner (D) determined that the sum of $487,647.46 ($511,192.50 less 4% discount rate) was taxable as ordinary income in 1951. The Tax Court held that all $511,192.50 was taxable for that year on the grounds that that amount could have been paid immediately and had a cash equivalency. Cowden (P) appealed.

ISSUE: If a promise to pay has the equivalency of cash, is it taxable in like manner as cash had it been received by the taxpayer rather than the obligation?

HOLDING AND DECISION: (Jones, J.) Yes. If a promise to pay of a solvent obligor is unconditional and assignable, not subject to set-offs, and is of a kind that is frequently transferred to lenders or investors at a discount not substantially greater than the generally prevailing premium for the use of money, such promise is the equivalent of cash and taxable in like manner as cash had cash been received by the taxpayer, rather than the obligation. While parties may contract in such manner so as to avoid or reduce taxation, if the consideration for which one of the parties bargains is the equivalent of cash it will be subjected to taxation to the extent of its fair market value. The equivalent of cash doctrine is applicable where the obligation to make deferred payments is represented by notes, bonds, or other evidence of indebtedness other than the contract. While the obligation here was evidenced by a writing other than the contract, it does not matter that it was not negotiable in form. Substance, not form, should be looked to. As the Tax Court gave great weight in reaching its decision to the willingness of Stanolind to pay rather than to the form of the transaction, the issue should be reconsidered according to the rule. Reversed and remanded.

EDITOR'S ANALYSIS: Upon the reasoning above, the Tax Court on remand reached the same conclusion as that originally appealed from, 20 T.C.M. 1134 (1961). Where a taxpayer received a note at a time when its maker was without funds, and the note could not be sold, its receipt was not the equivalent of cash and not taxable as income when received, even though it was eventually paid, 28 T.C. 1000 (1957). IRS has acquiesced to that holding. 1958-1 C.B. 6. Note that the cash equivalency doctrine ties in with the doctrine of constructive receipt. Above, it appeared that the Tax Court confused the two, leading to remand of the case.

[For more information on the cash equivalency doctrine, see Casenote Law Outline on Federal Income Taxation, Chapter 8, § II, Tax Accounting Methods.]

NOTES:

REED v. COMMISSIONER

723 F.2d 138 (1st Cir. 1983).

NATURE OF CASE: Appeal from Tax Court decision sustaining a notice of deficiency.

FACT SUMMARY: Reed (P) arranged for the money from his sale of shares in a company in 1973 to be paid the following year through an escrow arrangement.

CONCISE RULE OF LAW: Taxpayers may shift income recognition of a purchase-sale contract by deferred payment through an escrow arrangement if it is part of a bona fide arm's length agreement and the seller receives no present beneficial interest from the funds.

FACTS: Reed (P) agreed to sell his shares in a company to Cvengros for $808,500. It was agreed that the closing would take place on December 27, 1993, but Reed (P) did not want to receive the funds until 1974 for tax purposes. Thus, a modification to the contract was arranged whereby Reed (P) delivered the shares to Cvengros on the closing date but the money was deposited into escrow and not available to Reed (P) until January 3, 1974. After Reed (P) reported the income for the 1974 taxable year, the Commissioner (D) issued a notice of deficiency. The Tax Court agreed with the Commissioner (D) that the income was taxable in 1973 since Reed (P) had received an economic benefit in that year. Reed (P) appealed.

ISSUE: May taxpayers shift income recognition of a purchase-sale contract by deferred payment through an escrow arrangement if it is part of a bona fide arm's length agreement and the seller receives no present beneficial interest from the funds?

HOLDING AND DECISION: (Gibson, J.) Yes. Taxpayers may shift income recognition of a purchase-sale contract by deferred payment through an escrow arrangement if it is part of a bona fide arm's length agreement and the seller receives no present beneficial interest from the funds. The economic benefit doctrine has been used in prior decisions to hold escrow arrangements ineffective to defer income. The doctrine depends on two factors: (1) the taxpayer must receive some present, beneficial interest from the escrow account and (2) the escrow arrangement must be the product of the taxpayer's self-imposed limitation on funds that the taxpayer had an unqualified right to control. In the present case, neither of those factors apply to Reed's (P) contract with Cvengros. The sales contract was an arm's length agreement and Reed (P) had no control, or beneficial interest, over the funds while they were in escrow. Furthermore, an extension of the economic benefit doctrine to fit this case would erode the distinction between cash and accrual methods of accounting. Accordingly, Reed (P) should have been allowed to use the escrow arrangement to defer the income.

EDITOR'S ANALYSIS: The court also rejected the Commissioner's (D) argument that an agency relationship for income recognition purposes was established by the escrow arrangement. The court found that the escrowee bank was acting on behalf of both parties to the stock sale. To establish an agency relationship there must be a unilateral device set up by the taxpayer.

[For more information on cash method accounting, see Casenote Law Outline on Federal Income Taxation, Chapter 8, § II, Tax Accounting Methods.]

NOTES:

ZANINOVICH v. COMMISSIONER

616 F.2d 429 (9th Cir. 1980).

NATURE OF CASE: Appeal from the disallowment of a business expense.

FACT SUMMARY: Zaninovich (P) claimed that an advance lease payment mostly covering the next year was a business expense for the current year.

CONCISE RULE OF LAW: Expenditures are treated as capital expenses only if they create an asset having a useful life in excess of one year.

FACTS: Zaninovich (P), a commercial farmer, leased land for the period between December 1, 1973, and November 30, 1993. The yearly rent of $27,000 was payable on December 20, 1973. Zaninovich (P) deducted this entire $27,000 amount for the taxable year 1973. The Commissioner (D) disallowed $24,934 (representing 11/12 of the total). The Tax Court upheld the Commissioner's (D) decision, and Zaninovich (P) appealed.

ISSUE: Are expenditures always treated as capital expenses if they create an asset having a useful life into the next taxable year?

HOLDING AND DECISION: (Ferguson, J.) No. Expenditures are treated as capital expenses only if they create an asset having a useful life in excess of one year. Treasury Regulation 1.461 provides that cash basis taxpayers should deduct expenses in the year of payment. However, it also states that where an expenditure results in creation of an asset having a useful life extending substantially beyond the close of the taxable year, it may only be deductible in part. Section 263 of the Internal Revenue Code, using a similar standard, also disallows deductions for capital expenditures. Thus, the issue in the present case is whether the advance rental payment for eleven months of 1974 is considered substantially beyond the taxable year of 1973. Most other circuit courts have applied the "one-year rule." Under this rule, expenditures are considered capital expenses only if they create an asset having a useful life in excess of one year. The key advantage to this rule is the ease of application. Accordingly, Zaninovich (P) is entitled to deduct the entire rental payment as a business expense for 1973. Reversed.

EDITOR'S ANALYSIS: In a footnote, the court noted that the one-year rule is more of a guidepost than a rigid rule. The decision also noted that the other circuits had never applied the rule to rental payments. The court determined that there was no reason that it should not apply to land rental situations.

[For more information on cash method accounting, see Casenote Law Outline on Federal Income Taxation Chapter 8, § II, Tax Accounting Methods.]

NOTES:

GRYNBERG v. COMMISSIONER

83 T.C. 255 (1984).

NATURE OF CASE: Appeal from disallowment of expense deductions.

FACT SUMMARY: Grynberg (P) prepaid oil and gas leases that were not due until the following year, but deducted the expenses for the current taxable year.

CONCISE RULE OF LAW: Prepaid items are deductible only if there is actual payment for a substantial business reason and prepayment does not create a material distortion of the taxpayer's income in the year of prepayment.

FACTS: Grynberg (P) held many oil and gas leases during the years 1974 through 1979. Grynberg (P) was obligated to pay the lessors a specified annual fee if no drilling was commenced. This was called a "delay rental." Payment of the delay rental prevented termination of the lease where production had not yet begun. Grynberg (P) had a policy of making the delay rental payment in the month prior to the due date for the specific lease at issue. However, Grynberg (P) also adopted a policy of paying the February and March delay rentals in December, in addition to the delay rental due in the following January. Grynberg (P) then deducted these payments in the year they were made. The Commissioner (D) disallowed these deductions as nondeductible advance deposits.

ISSUE: Are prepaid items deductible if there is actual payment for a substantial business reason and prepayment does not create a material distortion of the taxpayer's income in the year of prepayment?

HOLDING AND DECISION: (Swift, J.) Yes. Prepaid items are deductible only if there is actual payment for a substantial business reason and prepayment does not create a material distortion of the taxpayer's income in the year of prepayment. Where the deductibility of prepaid items is based on §§ 162 and 446(b) of the Internal Revenue Code, a well-established three-prong test applies for cash method taxpayers. The first requirement is that there must be actual payment of the item. Refundable deposits do not qualify. The second requirement is that there must be a substantial business reason for making the prepayment. If the payment is made only to accelerate the tax deduction, it will not be allowed. The final requirement is that the prepayment may not cause a material distortion of the taxpayer's income in that year. In the present case, it is clear that Grynberg (P) failed the second requirement. There is no business reason for the prepayments in question. Accordingly, the deductions are disallowed.

EDITOR'S ANALYSIS: The court found that the second requirement was based upon the ordinary and necessary language of § 162. The court declined to express an opinion regarding the general one-year rule for advance payments under Income Tax Regulation 1-461. In Zaninovich v. Commissioner, 616 F.2d 429 (1980) the Ninth Circuit decided that advance payments were deductible as long as they did not create assets with useful lives in excess of one year.

[For more information on cash method accounting, see Casenote Law Outline on Federal Income Taxation, Chapter 8, § II, Tax Accounting Methods.]

NOTES:

CHAPTER 28
ACCRUAL METHOD ACCOUNTING

QUICK REFERENCE RULES OF LAW

1. **Choice of Accounting Methods.** Under the accrual basis of taxpayer accounting when the right to receive an amount becomes fixed, the right accrues rendering the amount taxable income. (Georgia School Book Depository, Inc. v. Commissioner)

   [For more information on the accrual method of accounting, see Casenote Law Outline on Federal Income Taxation, Chapter 8, § II, Tax Accounting Methods.]

2. **Choice of Accounting Methods.** Accrual basis taxpayers must include actual receipts in the taxable year if the receipts were paid for future services with no fixed time for performance. (Schlude v. Commissioner)

   [For more information on accrual method, see Casenote Law Outline on Federal Income Taxation, Chapter 8, § II, Tax Accounting Methods.]

3. **Choice of Accounting Methods.** Under the accrual method, an expense is deductible for the taxable year in which all the events have occurred that determine the fact and amount of the liability. (United States v. General Dynamics)

   [For more information on tax accounting methods, see Casenote Law Outline on Federal Income Taxation, Chapter 8, § II, Tax Accounting Methods.]

4. **Inventory Accounting.** Inventory accounting for tax purposes must conform with accepted practices and clearly reflect income. (Thor Power Tool Co. v. Commissioner)

   [For more information on inventory accounting, see Casenote Law Outline on Federal Income Taxation, Chapter 8, § II, Tax Accounting Methods.]

Notes

GEORGIA SCHOOL BOOK DEPOSITORY v. COMMISSIONER

1 T.C. 463 (1943).

NATURE OF CASE: Action for a redetermination of a deficiency assessment.

FACT SUMMARY: Georgia School Book Depository (Depository) (P) contended that its brokerage fees were not earned until payment and that payment would be made, therefore, the fees were not taxable until actually paid.

CONCISE RULE OF LAW: Under the accrual basis of taxpayer accounting when the right to receive an amount becomes fixed, the right accrues rendering the amount taxable income.

FACTS: The Depository (P) was a broker which received an 8% commission on all books purchased through it by the State of Georgia. It worked under an accrual method of accounting, and would receive books from the publisher and hold them in trust for the state, which would order the books through the Depository (P). Payment for the books could only come from the Free Textbook Fund created by state law from excise taxes on beer. In 1938 and 1939, the Depository (P) held certain books for the state, but did not receive payment due to a lack of money in the Fund. The IRS (D) assessed a deficiency against the Depository (P), contending its brokerage fees accrued and were, therefore, taxable in these years. The Depository (P) sued for a redetermination, contending the fees were not earned until payment and that there was no accrual because there was no reasonable expectancy that payment would ever be made.

ISSUE: Does an amount due under the accrual method of accounting become taxable when the right to receive it becomes fixed?

HOLDING AND DECISION: (Kern, J.) Yes. Under the accrual method of taxpayer accounting, when the right to receive an amount becomes fixed, the right accrues, rendering the amount taxable. In this case, the Depository (P) had done everything required of it to obtain payment in the taxable years in question. It received and stored the books and then distributed them to schools. As a result, its rights to payment became fixed, and, therefore, accrued, rendering it taxable. Further, the right to payment was not precluded from accruing because of the State's failure to immediately pay. There was no reason to believe that the prosperous State of Georgia would not eventually honor its obligation once the fund became solvent. Consequently, the payments accrued within the taxable years, rendering the Depository (P) liable for the taxes thereon. Judgment for the IRS (D).

EDITOR'S ANALYSIS: This case applies the "all events" test applicable in determining when accrual occurs. This test was first articulated in United States v. Anderson, 269 U.S. 422 (1939), in which it was held that an expense was deductible only in the year when all events which allow a determination of the amount of the liability occur. The test is codified in Regs. § 1.446-1(c)(1)(ii), as it applies to accrual of income, and Regs. § 1.461-1(a)(2) as it applies to expenses.

[For more information on the accrual method of accounting, see Casenote Law Outline on Federal Income Taxation, Chapter 8, § II, Tax Accounting Methods.]

NOTES:

SCHLUDE v. COMMISSIONER

372 U.S. 128 (1963).

NATURE OF CASE: Review of court of appeals judgment upholding notice of deficiency.

FACT SUMMARY: Schlude (P), the operator of a dance studio and an accrual basis taxpayer, did not include some income received in an earlier taxable year if a portion was for lessons in future years.

CONCISE RULE OF LAW: Accrual basis taxpayers must include actual receipts in the taxable year if the receipts were paid for future services with no fixed time for performance.

FACTS: Schlude (P) operated an Arthur Murray dance studio franchise. Lessons were offered under plans in which the customers made down payments and could receive the lessons at a future time. Schlude (P) was an accrual basis taxpayer. Under this accounting system, a deferred income account was credited for the total contract price when a customer started. At the close of the fiscal year, each customer's account was analyzed for the amount of lessons he had used. If the customer was entitled to additional lessons based on his prepayment, that amount was not declared as income for that year. If there was no customer activity for over a year, any amounts in the deferred account were then recognized as gain. The Commissioner (D) issued a notice of deficiency claiming that this accounting system did not clearly reflect the actual income received by Schlude (P) in a given year. The Tax Court and the court of appeals agreed, ruling for the Commisioner (D). Schlude (P) petitioned for certiorari, and the Supreme Court granted review.

ISSUE: Must accrual basis taxpayers include actual receipts in the taxable year if the receipts were paid for future services with no fixed time?

HOLDING AND DECISION: (White, J.) Yes. Accrual basis taxpayers must include actual receipts in the taxable year if the receipts are paid for future services with no fixed time for performance. Our decision in American Automobile Association v. United States, 367 U.S. 687, squarely controls this issue. In that case, the entire legislative history of the treatment of prepaid income was examined. Congress sought to grant deferral privileges to limited groups of taxpayers only. Our prior decision involved nearly the same practice as at issue in this case. We determined that where advance payments were related to services that were to be performed only upon customers' demands without relation to fixed dates, the income cannot be deferred. In the present case, Schlude (P) did not have fixed appointments for future lessons. Customers could demand lessons at any time in the future under their prepaid contracts. Therefore, these advance payments must be included as income in the taxable year they were received. Affirmed.

DISSENT: (Stewart, J.) The fixed date of performance standard has nothing to do with the aspect of the accounting system that the majority finds objectionable. The majority actually seems to favor a system whereby Schlude (P) would report income based upon estimated cancellations. While this would better estimate the actual income, it would have to be based on the same type of statistical evaluations this Court has already disapproved.

EDITOR'S ANALYSIS: The dissent correctly pointed out that this decision left Schlude (P) with hardly any options under an accrual basis method. The majority also approved the Commissioner's (D) decision to include in gross income payments to Schlude (P) by negotiable notes as well as cash. The majority noted that for accrual basis taxpayers it is the right to receive and not the actual receipt that determines income.

[For more information on accrual method, see Casenote Law Outline on Federal Income Taxation, Chapter 8, § II, Tax Accounting Methods.]

NOTES:

UNITED STATES v. GENERAL DYNAMICS

481 U.S. 239 (1987).

NATURE OF CASE: Appeal from disallowance of deductions.

FACT SUMMARY: General Dynamics (P) claimed deductions for employee medical payments for services that had been rendered, but did so before the employees submitted claims forms.

CONCISE RULE OF LAW: Under the accrual method, an expense is deductible for the taxable year in which all the events have occurred that determine the fact and amount of the liability.

FACTS: General Dynamics (P) became a medical care self-insurer for its employees. To receive reimbursement for covered medical services, employees submitted claims forms to GD (P) which verified and reviewed the claims before payment. Accordingly, there was a delay between the provision of medical services and payment by GD (P). Thus, GD (P) established a reserve account to reflect its liability for care received but not yet paid. For its 1972 tax return, GD (P) deducted its reserve account as an accrued expense. The IRS (D) disallowed the deduction but the Claims Court and the court of appeals ruled for GD (P). The IRS (D) appealed.

ISSUE: Under the accrual method, is an expense deductible for the taxable year in which all the events have occurred that determine the fact and amount of the liability?

HOLDING AND DECISION: (Marshall, J.) Yes. Under the accrual method, an expense is deductible for the taxable year in which all the events have occurred that determine the fact and amount of the liability. This court has established that whether a business expense has been incurred so as to entitle an accrual-basis taxpayer to deduct it under § 162(a) is governed by the "all events" test. This test provides that all of the events that determine the fact and amount of liability must have occurred in order for the expense to be deductible. Mere estimates of liability do not qualify; they must be firmly established. In the present case, the lower courts mistakenly found that the last event necessary to fix GD's (P) liability was the receipt of medical care by employees. Actually, GD (P) became liable only if properly documented claim forms were filed. Some employees may not have submitted forms for their services. Thus, a reserve based on the proposition that events are likely to occur may be an appropriate conservative accounting measure, but it does not warrant a tax deduction. Reversed.

EDITOR'S ANALYSIS: The principle outlined in this case goes back to United States v. Anderson, 269 U.S. 422 (1926). In that case, the Supreme Court ruled that a taxpayer had to deduct from his income a tax on profits from sales in that year. However, the tax would not be assessed and formally due until the following year.

[For more information on tax accounting methods, see Casenote Law Outline on Federal Income Taxation, Chapter 8, § II, Tax Accounting Methods.]

NOTES:

THOR POWER TOOL CO. v. COMMISSIONER

439 U.S. 522 (1979).

NATURE OF CASE: Appeal from disallowance of inventory write-down.

FACT SUMMARY: Thor Power (P) wrote down its excess inventory but did not immediately scrap the articles or sell them at reduced prices.

CONCISE RULE OF LAW: Inventory accounting for tax purposes must conform with accepted practices and clearly reflect income.

FACTS: Thor Power Tool (P) manufactured and sold power tools and parts. Thor (P) used the "lower cost or market" method of valuing its inventory for financial accounting and tax purposes. In 1964, Thor (P) decided that its inventory was overvalued and wrote down all of its excess inventory at once. However, the excess inventory was not scrapped or sold at reduced prices. Instead, it was retained and sold at the original prices because Thor (P) found that price reductions did not help the articles sell. The write-down of the excess inventory, however, reduced the amount of income for tax purposes. The Commissioner (D) disallowed the write-down, contending that it did not serve to accurately reflect Thor's (P) 1964 income. The Tax Court upheld this ruling, and Thor (P) appealed.

ISSUE: Must inventory accounting for tax purposes conform with accepted practices and clearly reflect income?

HOLDING AND DECISION: (Blackmun, J.) Yes. Inventory accounting for tax purposes must conform with accepted practices and clearly reflect income. Inventory accounting is governed by §§ 446 and 471 of the Internal Revenue Code, which provide that taxable income must be computed under the regular accounting method of the taxpayer and the method must clearly reflect income. These rules give the Commissioner (D) wide discretion in determining whether a particular method of inventory accounting is proper. There is no presumption that a generally accepted method is valid for tax purposes. In the present case, Thor (P) must value inventory for tax purposes at cost unless the market value is lower. Market value is defined as replacement cost unless the taxpayer can substantiate a lower valuation through evidence of actual sales or offerings. Without this type of objective evidence, a taxpayer's mere assertions as to market value are not relevant. In the present case, the excess inventory written down by Thor (P) was indistinguishable and intermingled with other inventory. Taxpayers may not write-down inventory on the basis of their own subjective valuations. Therefore, the Commissioner's disallowance must be upheld. Affirmed.

EDITOR'S ANALYSIS: The Court also rejected Thor's (P) argument that it was impossible to offer objective evidence of the excess inventory's lower value since it could not be sold at reduced prices. The Court held that Thor (P) simply had to choose between writing off the loss and take the tax benefit or wait and hope that the article would eventually sell. The Court saw no reason why Thor (P) should be able to hedge its bets.

[For more information on inventory accounting, see Casenote Law Outline on Federal Income Taxation, Chapter 8, § II, Tax Accounting Methods.]

NOTES:

CHAPTER 29
ANNUAL ACCOUNTING

QUICK REFERENCE RULES OF LAW

1. **Net Operating Losses.** Money earned is properly taxed to the period in which it is received, even if it is attributable to work performed in a previous taxable year. (Burnet v. Sanford and Brooks Company)

   [For more information on gross income, see Casenote Law Outline on Federal Income Taxation, Chapter 1, § III, Gross Income.]

2. **Net Operating Losses.** The return of charitable gifts is treated as income in the year of their recovery. (Alice Phelan Sullivan Corporation v. United States)

   [For more information on taxable year, see Casenote Law Outline on Federal Income Taxation, Chapter 8, § I, The Taxable Year.]

3. **Net Operating Losses.** The subsequent recovery of a previously deducted payment is not always necessary to invoke the tax benefit rule. (Hillsboro National Bank v. Commissioner)

   [For more information on annual accounting, see Casenote Law Outline on Federal Income Taxation, Chapter 8, § I, The Taxable Year.]

Notes

BURNET v. SANFORD AND BROOKS CO.

282 U.S. 359 (1931).

NATURE OF CASE: Appeal from reversal of Tax Court decision sustaining Commissioner's (D) assessment of a deficiency tax for income and profits.

FACT SUMMARY: Sanford and Brooks Co. (P) was paid under performance installments for a long-term dredging contract. Sanford and Brooks (P) brought suit when the contract was abandoned.

CONCISE RULE OF LAW: Money earned is properly taxed to the period in which it is received, even if it is attributable to work performed in a previous taxable year.

FACTS: Sanford and Brooks Co. (P) engaged in a long-term dredging operation. Payments were made each year by the other contracting party. Nonetheless, expenses exceeded payments by more than $176,000. A net operating loss was shown in 1913, 1915, and 1916. In 1915, the work was abandoned, and a suit was filed by Sanford and Brooks Co. (P) in 1916 against the other contracting party. Sanford and Brooks Co. (P) recovered their losses of $176,000 and $16,000 in interest. The Commissioner (D) assessed a delinquent tax for 1920, the year in which the suit was decided of $192,000. The court of appeals held that only the interest award of $16,000 should have been included in income. The $176,000 was merely a return of expenses previously incurred in 1913, 1915, and 1916. The Commissioner (D) appealed, claiming that the recovery was income, and the previous expenditures could not be considered.

ISSUE: Must all money that is received, excluding the sale of capital assets, in a given fiscal year be included in gross income?

HOLDING AND DECISION: (Stone J.) Yes. The money received was from a contract entered into for profit. Since no capital investments were involved, any money earned from the contract must equal gross income. The fact that no real profit was made on the contract is immaterial. The funds only become income when they are received. Net losses in previous periods have nothing to do with the current period. This rationale is consistent with the meaning and purpose of the Sixteenth Amendment. It is essential that any system of taxation produces ascertainable revenue payable at a given interval. The losses sustained could only be properly taken as deductions against income in those years. Subsequent "income" must be reported in the year it was received.

EDITOR'S ANALYSIS: Section 172 of the Code provides for a net operating loss carryback or carryover. Even if applicable, it would not have aided Sanford and Brooks Co. (P), because the income received in 1922 would have been received beyond the statutory period provided for in the Code, i.e., five years.

[For more information on gross income, see Casenote Law Outline on Federal Income Taxation, Chapter 1, § III, Gross Income.]

NOTES:

ALICE PHELAN SULLIVAN CORPORATION v. UNITED STATES

381 F.2d 399 (Claims Court 1967).

NATURE OF CASE: Action to recover alleged overpayment of tax.

NOTES:

FACT SUMMARY: Two parcels of property donated to charity by Alice Phelan Sullivan Corp. (P) were returned and taxed as income during the year of recovery.

CONCISE RULE OF LAW: The return of charitable gifts is treated as income in the year of their recovery.

FACTS: Alice Phelan Sullivan Corporation (P) donated two parcels of property to a charitable organization. During that year, Alice Phelan (P) claimed a charitable deduction and enjoyed a $1,877 tax benefit. In 1957, the property was returned to Alice Phelan. The Commissioner (D) viewed this transaction as adding $8,706 in income for 1957. Since the corporate tax rate for 1957 was 52%, the Commissioner (D) assessed a $4,527 deficiency. Alice Phelan (P) claimed that it should owe only the original tax benefit of $1,877 and petitioned for relief.

ISSUE: Is the return of charitable gifts treated as income in the year of their recovery?

HOLDING AND DECISION: (Collins, J.) Yes. The return of charitable gifts is treated as income in the year of their recovery. This court previously decided that in situations where prior charitable contributions are returned, the taxpayer should have to return the amount of the original tax benefit only at the time of donation. However, the principle that returned property is treated as income is well-ingrained in tax law. The only limitation is called the "tax-benefit" rule. This rule permits the exclusion of recovered items from income if the initial use as a deduction did not provide a tax saving. Section 111 of the Internal Revenue Code has codified these rules. In the present case, Alice Phelan (P) obtained full tax benefits from the earlier deductions. Therefore, the returned property was properly classified as income upon its recoupment and must be taxed at the 1957 rates. The previous decision by this court to the contrary is hereby overruled, and the petition is dismissed.

EDITOR'S ANALYSIS: The decision that was overruled in this case was Perry v. United States, 160 F. Supp. 270 (1958). The above opinion does not indicate why the Perry court deviated from the well-established rule outlined in this case. The basic case regarding annual accounting rules is Burnet v. Sanford & Brooks Co., 282 U.S. 359 (1931).

[For more information on taxable year, see Casenote Law Outline on Federal Income Taxation, Chapter 8, § I, The Taxable Year.]

HILLSBORO NATIONAL BANK v. COMMISSIONER

460 U.S. 370 (1983).

NATURE OF CASE: Appeal from deficiency notice.

FACT SUMMARY: The Commissioner (D) claimed that Hillsboro (P) should have reported as income a refunded tax for which Hillsboro (P) had taken a deduction.

CONCISE RULE OF LAW: The subsequent recovery of a previously deducted payment is not always necessary to invoke the tax benefit rule.

FACTS: Until 1970, Illinois imposed a property tax on shares held in banks. Banks were required to retain earnings sufficient to cover these taxes and customarily paid the taxes for the shareholders. The Internal Revenue Code allowed banks to deduct the tax amount. The shareholders were not allowed this deduction. In 1970, an amendment to the state constitution changed the law to prohibit ad valorem taxation of shares, but there was a long protracted battle over its legality. In the interim, the disputed taxes were placed in escrow. Hillsboro (P) paid the taxes for its shareholders in 1972 and took the deduction. Later, when the Supreme Court upheld the amendment, the County Treasurer refunded the taxes directly to the individual shareholders. When Hillsboro (P) did not recognize these events on its tax return, the Commissioner (D) assessed a deficiency contending that it should have included the refunded taxes as income. The Tax Court and the court of appeals affirmed, and Hillsboro (P) appealed.

ISSUE: Is the subsequent recovery of a previously deducted payment always necessary to invoke the tax payment rule?

HOLDING AND DECISION: (O'Connor, J.) No. The subsequent recovery of a previously deducted payment is not always necessary to invoke the tax benefit rule. The tax benefit rule is a judicially developed principle that allays some of the inflexibilities and transactional inequities of the annual accounting system. Often, completed transactions reopen unexpectedly in subsequent tax years. In order to avoid possible distortions of income, courts have long required taxpayers to recognize repayments of past deductions as income in the subsequent year. The basic purpose of the tax benefit rule is not to simply tax recoveries but to approximate the results of a transactional-based tax system. Accordingly, the rule cancels out an earlier deduction only when a careful examination shows that the later event is inconsistent with the deduction. In the present case, the Internal Revenue Code provision that allowed banks to take a deduction for their payments on behalf of their shareholders was focused on providing relief for the banks for their act of payment, rather than on the state's ultimate use of the tax. Therefore, the return of the money to the shareholders did not represent income to the banks, including Hillsboro (P). Reversed.

EDITOR'S ANALYSIS: The tax benefit rule started in the courts but was implicitly approved by Congress when it limited the rule by enacting § 111. Its purpose is to protect the government and the taxpayer from the adverse effects of reporting a transaction based on assumptions that a subsequent event proves to have been erroneous. But, not every unforeseen event will require a taxpayer to report income in the amount of this earlier deduction. Pursuant to the rule, the Commissioner may require a compensating recognition of income when an event occurs, but only if the occurrence of the event in the earlier year would have resulted in the disallowance of the deduction.

[For more information on annual accounting, see Casenote Law Outline on Federal Income Taxation, Chapter 8, § I, The Taxable Year.]

NOTES:

Notes

CHAPTER 30
CAPITAL GAINS AND LOSSES

QUICK REFERENCE RULES OF LAW

1. **Holding Period.** Capital gains treatment of real estate gains is available only to passive investors. (Bynum v. Commissioner)

   [For more information on capital gains, see Casenote Law Outline on Federal Income Taxation, Chapter 4, § V, Capital Gains and Losses.]

2. **Holding Period.** A taxpayer's motivation in purchasing an asset is irrelevant in determining whether the asset is a capital asset and thus subject to capital loss treatment. (Arkansas Best Corporation v. Commissioner)

   [For more information on capital asset definition, see Casenote Law Outline on Federal Income Taxation, Chapter 4, § V, Capital Gains and Losses.]

3. **Holding Period.** Where the unexpired portion of a lease is settled for cash, the payment received by the taxpayer is merely a substitute for rent and must be reported as ordinary income. (Hort v. Commissioner)

   [For more information on lease termination payments, see Casenote Law Outline on Federal Income Taxation, Chapter 4, § V, Capital Gains and Losses.]

4. **Holding Period.** While no gain is realized on the transfer by a testamentary, trustee of specific securities or other property bequeathed by will to a legatee, a pro tanto exchange of securities or other property to satisfy the general claim of a legatee is a "sale or disposition" and can result in such a gain. (Kenan v. Commissioner)

   [For more information on relief from debt obligations, see Casenote Law Outline on Federal Income Taxation, Chapter 4, § II, Amount Realized.]

Notes

BYNUM v. COMMISSIONER
46 T.C. 295 (1966).

NATURE OF CASE: Appeal from notice of deficiency.

FACT SUMMARY: The Bynums (P) sold subdivided lots on their property and sought to claim the income as long-term capital gains.

CONCISE RULE OF LAW: Capital gains treatment of real estate gains is available only to passive investors.

FACTS: Bynum (P) purchased land in 1942. Bynum (P) lived on the property and also conducted a nursery and landscaping business on the property. The business borrowed much money but was not profitable. Bynum (P), in an attempt to pay off the mortgage, improved and subdivided part of the property and advertised lots for sale as Morayshire Estates. The public was advised to contact Bynum (P) or a realtor. In 1960 and 1961, twenty lots were sold directly by Bynum (P). Bynum (P), who had continued to spend 90% of his time on the nursery business, then claimed the resulting income from the lot sales as capital gains profit. The Commissioner (D) asserted that the income was taxable as ordinary income since Bynum (P) was in the business of selling lots.

ISSUE: Is capital gains treatment available for all real estate gains?

HOLDING AND DECISION: (Forrester, J.) No. Capital gains treatment of real estate gains is available only to passive investors. Section 1221 of the Internal Revenue Code provides that property held by the taxpayer primarily for sale to customers in the ordinary course of trade or business creates regular income. Since the long-term capital gains provisions of the Code are an exception to normal tax rates, they must be construed narrowly and the taxpayer has the burden of proving their applicability. Each determination must be considered on the basis of the particular facts of the case. In the present case, the record shows that Bynum (P) was doing more than simply trying to get out of debt. Bynum (P) was attempting to subdivide up to 233 lots and personally conducted all of the improvement and promotional activities. This is not the posture of a passive investor. Bynum (P) was actively engaged in a second business. Thus, the property was being held primarily and principally for sale to customers in the ordinary course of this business. Therefore, income from these sales is not entitled to long-term capital gains treatment. The Commissioner (D) is affirmed.

CONCURRENCE: (Tannenwald, J.) This case shows that property profits are often partially attributable to both appreciation of value and the fruits of business. Some method of allocation should be created within an appropriate statutory framework.

EDITOR'S ANALYSIS: Sections 1231 and 1221 have identical language regarding property held for sale. In Burnet v. Harmel, 287 U.S. 103(1932), the Supreme Court held that capital gains treatment was reserved for appreciations in value over a substantial period of time. Capital gains are given preferential treatment because it may sometimes be a hardship to the taxpayers when gains accruing over years of value appreciation are all taxed in one year.

[For more information on capital gains, see Casenote Law Outline on Federal Income Taxation, Chapter 4, § V, Capital Gains and Losses.]

NOTES:

ARKANSAS BEST CORPORATION v. COMMISSIONER
485 U.S. 212 (1988).

NATURE OF CASE: Appeal from decision reversing Tax Court ruling that stock loss was not capital loss.

FACT SUMMARY: Arkansas Best Corporation (ABC) (P) appealed from a decision reversing the Tax Court's determination that a portion of its claimed stock loss was subject to ordinary loss treatment, contending that its purpose in acquiring and holding the stock was relevant to the determination of whether the stock was a capital asset.

CONCISE RULE OF LAW: A taxpayer's motivation in purchasing an asset is irrelevant in determining whether the asset is a capital asset and thus subject to capital loss treatment.

FACTS: ABC (P), a diversified holding company, began acquiring stock in the National Bank of Commerce in Dallas, Texas, in 1968. The Bank prospered until 1972, when it began to experience problems because of heavy real estate loans. ABC (P) continued to purchase stock in the Bank, prompted by the Bank's problems. In 1975 ABC (P) sold the bulk of its stock in the Bank and sought to take a $9,995,688 ordinary loss resulting from the sale on its 1975 tax return. The Commissioner (D) disallowed the deduction, characterizing the loss as a capital loss and not an ordinary loss. ABC (P) challenged the Commissioner's (D) decision in the U.S. Tax Court. The Tax Court found that ABC's (P) stock acquisitions after 1972 were made and held exclusively for business and not investment purposes, and therefore, relying on cases interpreting Corn Products Relining Co. v. Commissioner, 350 U.S. 46 (1955), accorded the loss realized on the sale of stock acquired after 1972 ordinary loss treatment. The court of appeals reversed the tax court, according the loss capital loss treatment, finding ABC's (P) motive in purchasing the stock irrelevant to the determination of whether the stock was a capital asset. From this decision, ABC (P) appealed.

ISSUE: Is a taxpayer's motivation in purchasing an asset relevant in determining whether an asset is a capital asset and thus subject to capital loss treatment?

HOLDING AND DECISION: (Marshall, J.) No. A taxpayer's motivation in purchasing an asset is irrelevant in determining whether the asset is a capital asset and thus subject to capital loss treatment. It can be assumed here that the stock was acquired and held for business and not investment purposes. Section 1221 of the Internal Revenue Code does not discuss motive, however, and the language of that section does signify that the listed exceptions to the definition of "capital asset" were meant to be exclusive. To read a motive test into the § 1221 capital asset determination would render the listed exceptions superfluous. ABC's (P) reliance on Corn Products is too great. That decision involves an application of § 1221's inventory exception. Since ABC (P) is not a dealer in securities, and has never suggested that the Bank stock falls within the inventory exception, Corn Products has no applicability to the present case. Today's holding prevents taxpayer abuse by keeping the taxpayer from taking capital gain treatment on profits and ordinary loss treatment on losses related to the sale of stocks, which are naturally viewed as a capital asset. Affirmed.

EDITOR'S ANALYSIS: The decision in the present case makes it clear that the nature of the asset, and not the asset's treatment motivation behind the asset's acquisition, determines the tax treatment accorded losses and profits from sales of such assets. The court's decision in the present case will restrict a trend towards expansive interpretations of the Com Products decision, which were resulting in any transaction integrally related to the taxpayer's business being given ordinary gain or loss treatment.

[For more information on capital asset definition, see Casenote Law Outline on Federal Income Taxation, Chapter 4, § V, Capital Gains and Losses.]

NOTES:

HORT v. COMMISSIONER

318 U.S. 28 (1941).

NATURE OF CASE: Appeal from circuit court's decision affirming Commissioner's (D) denial of a deduction for the value of the unexpired portion of a lease.

FACT SUMMARY: Hort (P) allowed a lease to be canceled in exchange for $140,000.

CONCISE RULE OF LAW: Where the unexpired portion of a lease is settled for cash, the payment received by the taxpayer is merely a substitute for rent and must be reported as ordinary income.

FACTS: Hort (P) was left a building under the terms of his father's will. One of the tenants, Irving Trust Co., wished to terminate the lease prior to its expiration date. They settled the lease by paying Hort (P) $140,000 in exchange for being released from it. Hort (P) did not report the $140,000 as income and claimed a deduction for the difference between the fair rental value of the space for the unexpired term of the lease and the $140,000 he received. The Commissioner (D) disallowed the deduction and assessed a deficiency tax on the $140,000. Hort (P) claimed that the $140,000 was a capital gain and even if it was ordinary income, he sustained a loss on the unexpired portion of the lease. The Tax Court and the circuit court sustained the Commissioner.

ISSUE: Where a lease is terminated prior to the expiration date and the taxpayer receives cash compensation, must it be reported as ordinary income?

HOLDING AND DECISION: (Murphy, J.) Yes. Hort (P) received the money, after negotiations, as a substitute for rent. Section 61 (a) would have required Hort (P) to include prepaid rent or an award for breach of contract as income. Hort (P) received an amount of money in lieu of the rental income he was entitled to under the lease. Since it was a substitute for ordinary income, it must be treated in the same manner. The consideration received by Hort (P) was not a return of capital. A lease is not considered a capital asset within the context of § 61(a). Further, the fact that Hort (P) received less than he would have under the terms of the lease does not entitle him to a deduction. No loss was sustained. He released a legal right for a settlement sum. Hort (P) didn't have to do so, and having made the decision to settle the amount realized by him must be deemed fair. Any injury to Hort (P) can only be fixed when the extent of the loss can be ascertained, i.e. when the property is re-rented. Until that time, no loss is deductible. The decision of the Commissioner (D) is sustained.

EDITOR'S ANALYSIS: In U.S. v. Dresser Industries, Inc., 324 F.2d 56 (5th Cir. 1963), the Court addressed itself to the "anticipated future income" problem. The Court held that the only commercial value of any property is the present worth of future earnings or usefulness. If the government can challenge a sale based on the fact that the sales price is only a substitute for future earnings, then no asset could qualify for capital gains treatment. The question of capital gains treatment really revolves around whether the present sale represents the right to "earn" future income or the right to "earned" future income.

[For more information on lease termination payments, see Casenote Law Outline on Federal Income Taxation, Chapter 4, § V, Capital Gains and Losses.]

NOTES:

KENAN v. COMMISSIONER

114 F.2d 217 (2nd Cir. 1940).

NATURE OF CASE: Cross-petitions seeking review of a determination that capital gain was realized.

FACT SUMMARY: Mrs. Bingham, the testatrix, provided in her will that Louise Wise would receive $5,000,000 when she reached 40. A proviso allowed the substitution of marketable securities of equal value, so part of the $5,000,000 was paid in that manner.

CONCISE RULE OF LAW: While no gain is realized on the transfer by a testamentary, trustee of specific securities or other property bequeathed by will to a legatee, a pro tanto exchange of securities or other property to satisfy the general claim of a legatee is a "sale or disposition" and can result in such a gain.

FACTS: A clause in the will of Mrs. Bingham, in which she left Louise Wise (her niece) an annual income and a $5,000,000 lump sum to be paid when she became 40, permitted the trustees to substitute securities of equal value in making certain payments (including that to Louise Wise). Mrs. Bingham's death in 1917 was followed later by the trustees' decision to pay part of Louise's allocation in securities (which they selected and valued in keeping with the will); this occurred when Louise reached 40 in 1935. All of the securities, most of which had been owned by the testator and became part of her estate and some of which the trustees had purchased, had appreciated. The Commissioner determined the distribution of same to Louise constituted a sale or exchange of capital assets and resulted in taxable capital gain. The Board overruled the trustees contention that no income of any character was realized and denied a motion by the Commissioner to amend his answer to assert all the gain was ordinary income. From this confirmation of the original deficiency determination of $367,687.12 both sides appeal, the Commissioner seeking a deficiency of $1,238,841.99.

ISSUE: When property is exchanged pro tanto to satisfy a legatee's general claim, does a sale or exchange of capital assets occur?

HOLDING AND DECISION: (Hand, J.) Yes. A satisfaction of a legatee's general claim against an estate via a pro tanto property exchange is not akin to the donative disposition that occurs via the transfer of specific property bequeathed by will to a legatee. The first is the sale or exchange of a capital asset with the rules concerning capital gains being applicable, while the latter is a donative transfer in which no gain is realized. Unlike a legacy of specific property, the instant legacy did not give title or right to the securities until they were delivered upon exercise of the trustee's option. Furthermore, Louise was not subject to the same chances that a specific property-legatee faces in dealing with the fluctuating value of same. The result was the same as if the securities were sold by the trustees and the $5,000,000 cash derived therefrom was used to pay Louise. In either case, a taxable capital gain is realized. Thus, the Board's decision is affirmed.

EDITOR'S ANALYSIS: The next case would seem to rest on an analysis which would alter the result in this case. However, the difference is that this case focuses on the debt-discharging obligor, while the next concentrates on the payment-receiving obligee. While recognizing how this shift changed the result, it should be noted that the rationale of the following case could have easily led to a rule that no exchange or sale results from this type of transaction regardless of the party upon whom the court focuses.

[For more information on relief from debt obligations, see Casenote Law Outline on Federal Income Taxation, Chapter 4, § II, Amount Realized.]

NOTES:

CHAPTER 31
QUASI-CAPITAL ASSETS: SECTION 1231

QUICK REFERENCE RULES OF LAW

1. **Recapture of Net Ordianry Losses: Section 1231(c).** Where sales are accepted, predictable, and are made in the ordinary course of business, they will not be accorded capital gain treatment, even though they were made as a last resort after trying to persuade customers to rent the items. (International Shoe Machine Corporation v. United States)

[For more information on capital gains and losses, see Casenote Law Outline on Federal Income Taxation, Chapter 4, § V, Capital Gains and Losses.]

Notes

INTERNATIONAL SHOE MACHINE CO. v. U.S.

F.2d (1st Cir. 1974)

NATURE OF CASE: Appeal from decision of Tax Court affirming Commissioner's (D) determination that property was held primarily for resale to customers.

FACT SUMMARY: International Shoe (P) rarely, until recently, sold machines but rather engaged in a highly profitable leasing business.

CONCISE RULE OF LAW: Where sales are accepted, predictable, and are made in the ordinary course of business, they will not be accorded capital gain treatment, even though they were made as a last resort after trying to persuade customers to rent the items.

FACTS: International Shoe (P) normally rented its machines to customers. Only a very small percentage of its income was from sales. In 1964, the purchase of machinery became attractive to customers because of the passage of the investment tax credit. The position of vice-president in charge of sales was created, price schedules were established, and discounts were offered to good customers. While customers were pressured in-so-far as was possible into renting, 271 machines were sold to those who had previously rented them. International Shoe (P) attempted to claim the income from the machines it sold as long-term capital gains. The Commissioner (0) determined that this was ordinary income from assets held primarily for customer resale in the ordinary course of business under § 1231(b)(1)(B). The Tax Court affirmed on the basis that this was an accepted and predictable portion of International Shoe's (P) business after the passage of the investment tax credit and that the machines were held primarily for resale to customers.

ISSUE: Where a taxpayer tries to rent its machinery but is forced to sell some of it to customers who want to buy, should the sale proceeds be treated as capital gains?

HOLDING AND DECISION: (Coffin, C.J.) No. The fact that International Shoe (P) wanted to rent its machines is not determinative. After the investment tax credits passage International Shoe (P) knew that some of its customers would want to buy the machines. It established the office of vice-president in charge of sales and performed other acts establishing that it expected to be selling machines. This was not a liquidation sale but was made in the ordinary course of International Shoe's (P) business. This sale rationale satisfies the "held primarily for sale to customers" requirement of § 1231. Customers, albeit reluctantly, were given the choice as to whether they wished to rent or buy. Therefore, machines that were sold were held primarily for sale to customers. The word "primarily" refers to an ongoing business purpose rather than a liquidation of interest as found in Malat v. Riddell, 383 U.S. 569(1966). International Shoe's (P) other argument is that these machines were no longer useful as rental equipment. The sale of rental-obsolescent equipment generally yields capital gains. However, there is no showing here that the machines could not be used for rental. Hence, this argument must fail. The decision of the Commissioner (D) is sustained.

EDITOR'S ANALYSIS: In Ridgewood Land Co. v. Commissioner, 477 F.2d 135 (5th Cir. 1973), it was held that land purchased for development and sale in the ordinary course of taxpayer's business became "investment property" when the development plans were abandoned because the land was condemned for a public purpose and thereafter held "for investment." The Court in International Shoe stated that, even though a sale may be "accepted and predictable," it may not be made in the ordinary course of business, e.g., a final liquidation of inventory. Therefore, both portions of the test must be met in order to find that the property was held primarily for sale to customers.

[For more information on capital gains and losses, see Casenote Law Outline on Federal Income Taxation, Chapter 4, § V, Capital Gains and Losses.]

NOTES:

NOTES

CHAPTER 33*
ASSIGNMENT OF INCOME

QUICK REFERENCE RULES OF LAW

1. **Use of Trusts to Shift Income.** A statute can tax salaries to those who earned them and can provide that a tax cannot be escaped by anticipatory arrangements or contracts which prevent salary from vesting even for a second in the person who earned it. (Lucas v. Earl)

   [For more information on income from services, see Casenote Law Outline on Federal Income Taxation, Chapter 9, § II, Attribution of Income and Deductions.]

2. **Use of Trusts to Shift Income.** For income tax purposes the power to dispose of income is the equivalent of ownership of it, and the exercise of that power to transfer payment of the income to another is the equivalent of realization of the income. (Helvering v. Horst)

   [For more information on the power to control income, see Casenote Law Outline on Federal Income Taxation, Chapter 9, § III, Preventing Assignment of Income and Deductions.]

3. **Use of Trusts to Shift Income.** Renewal commissions assigned by the taxpayer are taxable to the taxpayer in the year in which they become payable. (Helvering v. Eubank)

   [For more information on income from services, see Casenote Law Outline on Federal Income Taxation, Chapter 9, § II, Attribution of Income and Deductions.]

4. **Use of Trusts to Shift Income.** The true nature of a transaction, rather than formalisms, determines the tax consequences. (Salvatore v. Commissioner)

   [For more information on recognition of gains, see Casenote Law Outline on Federal Income Taxation, Chapter 4, § IV, Recognition of Gains and Losses.]

5. **Use of Trusts to Shift Income.** A taxpayer stockholder may assign his rights to anticipated dividends to avoid tax liability so long as the assignment is a bona fide, good-faith commercial transaction. (Stranahan v. Commissioner)

   [For more information on the "anticipatory-assignment-of-income doctrine," see Casenote Law Outline on Federal Income Taxation, Chapter 9, § III, Preventing Assignment of Income and Deductions.]

6. **Use of Trusts to Shift Income.** In a gift-leaseback situation, rental payments are deductible if the transfer was irrevocable and the benefits inure to the trust. (May v. Commissioner)

   [For more information on deductibility of expenses, see Casenote Law Outline on Federal Income Taxation, Chapter 7, § I, Expenses Relating to the Production of Income as Opposed to Those Relating to Personal Consumption.]

***There are no cases in Chapter 32.**

Notes

LUCAS v. EARL

281 U.S. 111 (1930).

NATURE OF CASE: On writ of certiorari to review a decision of the Tax Court.

NOTES:

FACT SUMMARY: The Earls (D) entered into a contract whereby they agreed that whatever each acquired in any way during their marriage would be received and owned by them as joint tenants. Hence Mr. Earl (D) claimed he could be taxed for only half of his income.

CONCISE RULE OF LAW: A statute can tax salaries to those who earned them and can provide that a tax cannot be escaped by anticipatory arrangements or contracts which prevent salary from vesting even for a second in the person who earned it.

FACTS: The Earls (D) entered into a contract whereby they agreed that whatever each acquired in any way during their marriage would be received and owned by them as joint tenants. Mr. Earl (D) claimed that due to the contract he could only be taxed for one half of his income for 1920 and 1921. The validity of the contract was not questioned.

ISSUE: Can an anticipatory contract prevent a salary from vesting, for tax purposes, in the person who earned it?

HOLDING AND DECISION: (Holmes, J.) No. Section 213(a) imposes a tax upon the net income of every individual including income derived from salaries, wages, or compensation for personal service of whatever kind and in whatever form paid. There is no doubt that the statute could tax salaries as to those who earned them. The tax could not be escaped by anticipatory arrangements and contracts however skillfully devised to prevent the salary from vesting even for a second in the person who earned it. This is true whatever the motives for the contract might have been.

EDITOR'S ANALYSIS: The Earls lived in California. Under that State's community property laws the wife did not have a vested interest in the husband's earnings until 1927. In Commissioner v. Harmon, 323 U.S. 44, the Court held a 1939 Oklahoma statute permitting spouses to elect to be governed by a community property system was not effective for federal income taxation. The Court said that the existence of an option resulted in a status similar to that in Lucas v. Earl and distinguished Poe v. Seaborn, where "the Court was not dealing with a consensual community, but one made an incident of marriage by the inveterate policy of the state." The dissent argued that Lucas v. Earl and Poe v. Seaborn state competing theories of income tax liability.

[For more information on income from services, see Casenote Law Outline on Federal Income Taxation, Chapter 9, § II, Attribution of Income and Deductions.]

HELVERING v. HORST

311 U.S. 112 (1940).

NOTES:

NATURE OF CASE: On writ of certiorari to review a reversal of a Tax Court decision.

FACT SUMMARY: Shortly before their due date, Horst (D) detached negotiable interest coupons from negotiable bonds and gave them to his son who in the same year collected them at maturity.

CONCISE RULE OF LAW: For income tax purposes the power to dispose of income is the equivalent of ownership of it, and the exercise of that power to transfer payment of the income to another is the equivalent of realization of the income.

FACTS: Horst (D) owned some negotiable bonds from which he detached the negotiable interest coupons shortly before their due date and gave them to his son. The son, in the same year, collected them at maturity. The Commissioner claimed that the interest payments were taxable to Horst (D).

ISSUE: Will a donor be taxed for interest payments on negotiable interest coupons which he detached, shortly before they were due, from negotiable bonds and gave to a donee who collected them at maturity in the same year?

HOLDING AND DECISION: (Stone, J.) Yes. The power to dispose of income is the equivalent of ownership of it. The exercise of that power to procure the payment of income to another is the enjoyment and hence the realization of the income by he who exercises it. The owner of negotiable bonds stands in the place of the lender. When by the gift of the coupons he separates his right to interest payments, as Horst (D) did here, and procures the payment of the interest to the donee, he enjoys the economic benefits of the income in the same manner and to the same extent as though the transfer were of earnings, and in either case, the fruit is not to be attributed to a different tree from that on which it grew.

EDITOR'S ANALYSIS: If the doctrine of Horst were applied literally a donor who gave Blackacre in 1930 might still be taxed on the income from it in 1960. On the other hand, the doctrine of Blair, which holds that where ownership of property is transferred the income arising therefrom cannot be taxed to the donor, has been criticized as restricting taxation of the donor too narrowly, since every inchoate right to past or future income may be said to be "property." In Horst, the Court distinguished Blair on the nature of the gift and the income transferred, frequently a determining issue.

[For more information on the power to control income, see Casenote Law Outline on Federal Income Taxation, Chapter 9, § III, Preventing Assignment of Income and Deductions.]

HELVERING v. EUBANK

311 U.S. 122 (1940).

NATURE OF CASE: Appeal from decision finding commissions taxable income.

FACT SUMMARY: The Government (D) appealed from a decision upholding Eubank's (P) position that renewal commissions assigned by Eubank (P) were not taxable in the year in which they became payable.

CONCISE RULE OF LAW: Renewal commissions assigned by the taxpayer are taxable to the taxpayer in the year in which they become payable.

FACTS: Eubank (P) was a life insurance agent. After the termination of his agency contracts and services as an agent, he assigned renewal commissions to become payable for services rendered before his termination. The Commissioner (D) assessed the renewal commissions paid to the assignees as income to Eubank (P) in the year they became payable. Eubank (P) challenged this tax treatment, and from a decision holding that the commissions assigned by Eubank (P) were not taxable to him in the year they became payable, the Commissioner (D) appealed.

ISSUE: Are renewal commissions assigned by the taxpayer taxable to the taxpayer in the year they become payable?

HOLDING AND DECISION: (Stone, J.) Yes. Renewal commissions assigned by the taxpayer are taxable to the taxpayer in the year in which they become payable. Reversed.

SEPARATE OPINION: (McReynolds, J.) Upon assignment of the commissions, Eubank (P) could do nothing further with respect to them. In no sense were they earned or received by him during the taxable year. The court below was correct in stating that when a taxpayer who makes his income tax on a cash basis assigns a right to monies payable in the future for work already performed, he transfers a property right, and the money when paid is not taxable to the taxpayer in the year paid.

EDITOR'S ANALYSIS: Future commissions such as those involved in the present case involve an element of interest on the amount of the commission earned. Issues can arise to what amount to be taxed, whether it should be the present value of the commission assigned, or the face value of the amount of the commissions at the time of the assignment.

[For more information on income from services, see Casenote Law Outline on Federal Income Taxation, Chapter 9, § II, Attribution of Income and Deductions.]

NOTES:

SALVATORE v. COMMISSIONER

T.C. Memo 1970-30.

NATURE OF CASE: Appeal from notice of deficiency for failure to fully report gain.

FACT SUMMARY: Salvatore (P) conveyed half of her gas station to her children as a gift just prior to selling it.

CONCISE RULE OF LAW: The true nature of a transaction, rather than formalisms, determines the tax consequences.

FACTS: Salvatore's (P) husband died and left his gas station to her. Salvatore's (P) children operated the station for several years before deciding to sell the property to Texaco for $295,000. The family decided that the proceeds from the sale would first be used to satisfy outstanding liabilities of the property. Then it was decided that Salvatore (P) would need approximately $100,000 to provide income for the rest of her life and that the balance would be divided among the children. Thus, Salvatore (P) conveyed a one-half interest in the property as a gift to her children just prior to the sale. Salvatore (P) reported the gifts on her tax return and paid a gift tax and then paid long-term capital gains taxes on her half of the sale proceeds. Her children paid gains taxes on their portions. The Commissioner (D) issued a notice of deficiency, maintaining that Salvatore (P) should actually pay capital gains taxes on the entire proceeds.

ISSUE: Does the true nature of a transaction, rather than formalisms, determine the tax consequences?

HOLDING AND DECISION: (Featherston, J.) Yes. The true nature of a transaction, rather than formalisms, determines the tax consequences. The Supreme Court in Commissioner v. Court Holding Co., 324 U.S. 331 (1945) established that taxation depends upon the substance of transactions. Tax consequences that arise from the sale of property are not determined solely by the means employed to transfer title. A sale by one person cannot be transformed into a sale by another by using the latter as a conduit through which to pass title. In the present case, Salvatore (P) owned the property outright. Her subsequent conveyance, unsupported by consideration, was actually only an intermediate step in the sale to Texaco. The children were conduits through which to pass title. The fact that the conveyance was a bona fide gift is immaterial in determining the tax consequences of the sale. Salvatore's (P) tax liabilities cannot be altered by a rearrangement of the legal title after the sale was already contracted. Therefore, all of the gain on the sale was properly taxable to Salvatore (P).

EDITOR'S ANALYSIS: This decision simply means that Salvatore (P) and her children will have to amend their returns. Salvatore (P) will still be liable for the gift tax, but her children will not owe capital gains tax. The principle of this case may prove difficult to apply when more complicated transactions are involved.

[For more information on recognition of gains, see Casenote Law Outline on Federal Income Taxation, Chapter 4, § IV, Recognition of Gains and Losses.]

NOTES:

ESTATE OF STRANAHAN v. COMMISSIONER
472 F.2d 867 (6th Cir. 1973).

NATURE OF CASE: Action against Commissioner for notice of deficiency of taxes.

FACT SUMMARY: Decedent Stranahan (P) assigned his rights to anticipated dividends to avoid tax liability.

CONCISE RULE OF LAW: A taxpayer stockholder may assign his rights to anticipated dividends to avoid tax liability so long as the assignment is a bona fide, good-faith commercial transaction.

FACTS: Decedent Stranahan (P), after paying the IRS more than $750,000 in back taxes, attempted to accelerate his income so that he could take full advantage of the interest deduction. He therefore assigned his rights to anticipated dividends in certain stocks to his son in consideration of $115,000. The dividends actually received by the son amounted to $40,000. On these facts, the Commissioner (D) claimed a deficiency of taxes based on the dividends to decedent Stranahan's estate (P). The Tax Court concluded that decedent Stranahan's (P) assignment of future dividends in exchange for the present discounted value of those dividends, although conducted in the form of an assignment of a property right, was in reality a loan to decedent Stranahan (P) masquerading as a sale and so disguised lacked any business purpose. Therefore, decedent Stranahan (P) realized taxable income when the dividend was declared.

ISSUE: May a stockholder assign his rights to anticipated dividends in exchange for the present discounted value of those dividends so that the stockholder transferor may avoid tax liability?

HOLDING AND DECISION: (Peck, J.) Yes. A stockholder may assign his rights to anticipated dividends in exchange for the present discounted value of those dividends in order to avoid tax liability. The only limitation is that the assignment must be a good-faith, bona fide commercial transaction. In this case, the transaction was economically realistic. The facts establish that decedent Stranahan (P) did in fact receive payment from his assignee, the son. Decedent Stranahan (P) completely divested himself of any interest in the dividends and vested that interest to his assignee son. We conclude that the Tax Court below was in error in not giving effectiveness to decedent Stranahan's (P) plan.

EDITOR'S ANALYSIS: The principal case is a departure from the general rule that income is chargeable to the person rendering the service for which income is paid or owning property from which the income is earned. Note also that the result in the case would have been different if decedent Stranahan (P) had attempted to make a gratuitous assignment or if the court would have felt that the assignment was not a bona fide commercial transaction.

[For more information on the "anticipatory-assignment-of-income doctrine," see Casenote Law Outline on Federal Income Taxation, Chapter 9, § III, Preventing Assignment of Income and Deductions.]

NOTES:

MAY v. COMMISSIONER

723 F.2d 1434 (9th Cir. 1984).

NATURE OF CASE: Appeal from Tax Court decision allowing business expense deductions.

FACT SUMMARY: May (P) deeded property to an irrevocable trust for the benefit of his children and then leased back the property from the trust.

CONCISE RULE OF LAW: In a gift-leaseback situation, rental payments are deductible if the transfer was irrevocable and the benefits inure to the trust.

FACTS: May (P), a doctor, deeded his entire interest in a parcel of real estate to an irrevocable trust for the benefit of his children. The trust instrument appointed a friend, Gross, as co-trustee. May (P) then rented the property from the trust for $1,000 a month under an oral lease to conduct his medical practice there. May (P) claimed the rent payment as an ordinary and necessary business expense deduction. The Commissioner (D) maintained that the deduction should be disallowed under the circumstances, but the Tax Court agreed with May (P). The Commissioner (D) appealed.

ISSUE: In a gift-leaseback situation, are rental payments deductible if the transfer was irrevocable and the benefits inure to the trust?

HOLDING AND DECISION: (Pregerson, J.) Yes. In a gift-leaseback situation, rental payments are deductible if the transfer was irrevocable and the benefits inure to the trust. The question of whether rental payments in a gift-leaseback situation are deductible under § 162(a)(3) is a frequently litigated issue. The Tax Court and the courts of appeals have developed different but similar standards. The Ninth Circuit has established that the fundamental issue is the sufficiency of the property interest transferred. Four factors must be considered in assessing the transfer: (1) the duration of the transfer; (2) controls retained by the donor; (3) use of the property for the benefit of the donor; and (4) independence of the trustee. In the present case, May (P) donated the property to an irrevocable trust, did not retain the same control over the property as before the gift, and used the property only as a lessee. Co-trustee Gross might have devoted more time to supervising the trust, but appeared to be independent of May (P). Therefore, May (P) is allowed to deduct the rental payment as a business expense. Affirmed.

EDITOR'S ANALYSIS: The court noted that some courts of appeals allow the deduction only if there was a business purpose for the entire transaction. Other circuits first look at the validity of the transfer and then examine the business purpose of the leaseback alone. The approach adopted by the Ninth Circuit requires only that the transfer be grounded in economic reality.

[For more information on deductibility of expenses, see Casenote Law Outline on Federal Income Taxation, Chapter 7, § I, Expenses Relating to the Production of Income as Opposed to Those Relating to Personal Consumption.]

NOTES:

CHAPTER 36*
TAX CONSEQUENCES OF DIVORCE

QUICK REFERENCE RULES OF LAW

1. **Legal Expenses.** Transfers of appreciated property pursuant to divorce in return for a release of marital rights are taxable events. (United States v. Davis)

   [For more information on recognition of gains, see Casenote Law Outline on Federal Income Taxation, Chapter 4, § IV, Recognition of Gains and Losses.]

2. **Legal Expenses.** Nonrecognition of gains for transfers of property to third parties incident to divorce applies only if the transfer is on behalf of a former spouse. (United States v. Blatt)

3. **Legal Expenses.** Litigation costs for resisting a claim are deductible only if the claim arises in connection with the taxpayer's profit-seeking activities. (United States v. Gilmore)

   [For more information on recognition of gains, see Casenote Law Outline on Federal Income Taxation, Chapter 4, § IV, Recognition of Gains and Losses.]

*** There are no cases in Chapter 34 or 35.**

Notes

UNITED STATES v. DAVIS

370 U.S. 65 (1962).

NATURE OF CASE: Review of reversal of deficiency notice for failure to report appreciated property.

FACT SUMMARY: Davis (P) transferred stock to his exwife pursuant to a divorce settlement, but did not report the stock appreciation.

CONCISE RULE OF LAW: Transfers of appreciated property pursuant to divorce in return for a release of marital rights are taxable events.

FACTS: In 1954, Davis (P) agreed to a divorce settlement whereby he agreed to transfer 1,000 shares of stock in E.I. du Pont de Nemours & Co. to his exwife. She accepted the division in full settlement of any claims and rights she had. The cost basis for the stock transferred was about $8,000 less than its market value at the time of the transfer. Davis (P) did not recognize this gain on his tax return, and the Commissioner (D) claimed a deficiency. The Court of Claims, however, ruled for Davis (P) and the Commissioner (D) appealed.

ISSUE: Are transfers of appreciated property pursuant to divorce in return for a release of marital rights taxable events?

HOLDING AND DECISION: (Clark, J.) Yes. Transfers of appreciated property pursuant to divorce in return for a release of marital rights are taxable events. The Internal Revenue Code mandates that all gains derived from dealings in property are deemed income. The critical question is when the appreciation of property must be recognized as a gain. Generally, gains must be recognized upon "sale or other disposition." In a divorce settlement, the rights of a spouse to the other's personal property do not reach the level of co-ownership. That spouse will have no interest over the management or disposition of the other spouse's property. Therefore, the transfer of property more closely resembles an exchange for release of a legal obligation. Furthermore, it is not true that it is impossible to compute the fair market value of released marital rights. It should be assumed that the rights are equal to the property exchanged for them. In the instant case, Davis (P) transferred the stock in return for which his wife agreed to give up her marital rights to alimony and other benefits. Therefore, his gain on the appreciated stock must be recognized at the time of the transfer. Reversed.

EDITOR'S ANALYSIS: In Philadelphia Park Amusement Co. v. United States, 126 F. Supp. 184 (1954), the Court of Claims established one of the principles cited in the above case. Absent a readily ascertainable value of property, it is presumed that exchanged properties are equal in value. This decision was in accord with the practice of most local courts.

[For more information on recognition of gains, see Casenote Law Outline on Federal Income Taxation, Chapter 4, § IV, Recognition of Gains and Losses.]

NOTES:

UNITED STATES v. BLATT
102 T.C. No. 5 (1994).

NATURE OF CASE: Appeal from notice of deficiency.

NOTES:

FACT SUMMARY: Ms. Blatt (P) redeemed her stock from a corporation owned equally by her husband, Mr. Blatt, when they divorced and then sought nonrecognition of the gain.

CONCISE RULE OF LAW: Nonrecognition of gains for transfers of property to third parties incident to divorce applies only if the transfer is on behalf of a former spouse.

FACTS: Ms. Blatt (P) divorced her husband, Mr. Blatt, in 1987. Pursuant to the divorce decree, Ms. Blatt (P) redeemed her stock in the company she and Mr. Blatt owned equally. The redemption produced $45,000 for Ms. Blatt (P), and the Commissioner (D) determined that she realized a long-term capital gain of $39,000. Ms. Blatt (P) claimed that this gain was entitled to nonrecognition as a transfer between former spouses under § 1041.

ISSUE: Does the nonrecognition of gains for transfers of property to third parties incident to divorce apply only if the transfer is on behalf of a former spouse?

HOLDING AND DECISION: (Laro, J.) Yes. Nonrecognition of gains for transfers of property to third parties incident to divorce applies only if the transfer is on behalf of a former spouse. Section 1041 of the Internal Revenue Code provides a broad rule of nonrecognition for sales, gifts, and other transfers of property between spouses or former spouses incident to divorce. The section addresses only transfers between spouses and does not include transfers to third parties, such as corporations. The basic policy is to treat husbands and wives as one economic unit and to defer the recognition of gains on interspousal property transfers until property is conveyed outside the unit. The regulations prescribed for § 1041 apply the tax-free treatment to certain transfers to third parties when they are on behalf of the former spouse incident to divorce. In the present case, Ms. Blatt's (P) transfer of stock to the corporation was not on behalf of Mr. Blatt. The redemption was a transaction between Ms. Blatt (P) and the corporation. She was not acting in the interest of, or as representative for, Mr. Blatt at the time of the redemption. Only transfers that satisfy an obligation of someone is a transfer on behalf of that person. Any putative benefit to Mr. Blatt, such as relief from possible claims under marital distribution laws, does not make the transfer on his behalf. Accordingly, the redemption was not a qualifying transfer under § 1041 and the long-term capital gain must be recognized.

EDITOR'S ANALYSIS: The regulation to § 1041 that established the "on behalf of" standard is § 1.1041-1T, Q&A 9. Petitioner relied on the case of Arnes v. United States, 981 F.2d 456 (9th Cir. 1992) where the court found that similar transfers benefited the former spouse because they limited future community property claims. The decision above disapproved of Arnes and also noted that it was easily distinguishable from the instant case since the husband in Arnes was the sole owner of the company.

UNITED STATES v. GILMORE
372 U.S. 39 (1963).

NATURE OF CASE: Review of allowance of deductions for litigation costs.

NOTES:

FACT SUMMARY: Gilmore (P) sought to deduct the costs of his successful defense of his wife's claims during divorce proceedings.

CONCISE RULE OF LAW: Litigation costs for resisting a claim are deductible only if the claim arises in connection with the taxpayer's profit-seeking activities.

FACTS: Gilmore's (P) wife brought a divorce action and claimed that Gilmore's (P) interests in three companies were community property. Gilmore (P) spent $40,000 successfully defending his wife's claims. He subsequently sought to deduct the expense from his federal income taxes because it was incurred for the conservation of property held for the production of income. The Court of Claims allowed Gilmore (P) to deduct 80% of the litigation costs, and the federal government (D) appealed.

ISSUE: Are all litigation costs for resisting claims deductible?

HOLDING AND DECISION: (Harlan, J.) No. Litigation costs for resisting a claim are deductible only if the claim arises in connection with the taxpayer's profit-seeking activities. Section 212 of the Internal Revenue Code allows for the deductibility of expenses for the conservation of property held for income. However, deductibility of these expenses depends on the origin and nature of the claims themselves, not the consequences of a successful claim. Legal expenses do not become deductible merely because they are paid for services that relieve a taxpayer of a liability. The legal claim must arise in connection with the business at issue. The fact that the claim would affect the taxpayer's income-producing property is not relevant. In the present case, Gilmore (P) was defending claims of a personal nature. The divorce proceedings had no connection with the business interests of Gilmore (P) other than the consequences. Accordingly, Gilmore's (P) litigation expenses were not deductible. Reversed and remanded.

EDITOR'S ANALYSIS: This decision resolved a conflict in the lower courts on the issue. The Court decided that § 212 deduction rules should mirror those of § 162 business expenses. Each excludes personal and family expenses.

[For more information on recognition of gains, see Casenote Law Outline on Federal Income Taxation, Chapter 4, § IV, Recognition of Gains and Losses.]

Notes

CHAPTER 37
NONRECOURSE DEBT: BASIS AND AMOUNT REALIZED REVISITED

QUICK REFERENCE RULES OF LAW

1. **Impact of Contingent Liabilities.** In computing basis, it is the fair market value of the property rather than the purchaser's equity which determines basis. (Crane v. Commissioner)

   [For more information on acquisition indebtedness, and the "Crane doctrine," see Casenote Law Outline on Federal Income Taxation, Chapter 4, § I, Basis.]

2. **Impact of Contingent Liabilities.** The assumption of a non-recourse mortgage constitutes a taxable gain to the mortgagor even if the mortgage exceeds the fair market value of the property. (Commissioner v. Tufts)

   [For more information on nonrecourse debts, see Casenote Law Outline on Federal Income Taxation, Chapter 4, § II, Amount Realized.]

3. **Impact of Contingent Liabilities.** Depreciation is not predicated upon ownership of property but rather upon an investment in property. (Estate of Franklin v. Commissioner)

   [For more information on acquisition indebtedness, see Casenote Law Outline on Federal Income Taxation, Chapter 4, § I, Basis.]

4. **Impact of Contingent Liabilities.** Interest and depreciation deductions are not allowed for nonrecourse indebtedness that exceeds the fair market value of the property purchased. (Pleasant Summit Land Corporation v. Commissioner; Prussin v. Commissioner)

   [For more information on nonrecourse debt, see Casenote Law Outline on Federal Income Taxation, Chapter 4, § I, Basis.]

5. **Impact of Contingent Liabilities.** The "amount realized" on a foreclosure sale under § 1001 of the Internal Revenue Code is represented by the proceeds of the sale. (Aizawa v. Commissioner)

   [For more information on nonrecourse debt, see Casenote Law Outline on Federal Income Taxation, Chapter 4, § I, Basis.]

NOTES

CRANE v. COMMISSIONER

331 U.S. 1 (1947).

NATURE OF CASE: Action challenging the basis assigned to property.

FACT SUMMARY: Crane (P) inherited real property subject to an unassumed mortgage.

CONCISE RULE OF LAW: In computing basis, it is the fair market value of the property rather than the purchaser's equity which determines basis.

FACTS: Crane (P) inherited an apartment building. The building had a mortgage on it which when combined with unpaid interest exactly equaled the estate tax appraiser's valuation of the building and property. Crane (P) did not assume the mortgage. She (P) agreed to remit the net rental proceeds after taxes to the mortgagor. Some six years later, forced with the threat of foreclosure, Crane (P) sold the property and received $2,500 in cash for it (net). Crane (P) included $1,250 in her income for the year on the theory that the property was a capital asset; her original basis in the property was zero; and, therefore, one-half the profits had to be included as income from the sale of a capital asset. The Commissioner (D) levied a deficiency tax. He claimed that her basis was the fair market price at the time of acquisition less allowable depreciation. Therefore, Crane (P) actually realized a gain of $2,500 in cash plus six years of depreciation deductions, a total of $23,767.03. Crane (P) argued that only her equity in the property could be considered as her basis. Since it was zero to begin with, no depreciation was allowed. Since she only realized $2,500 in cash, this was all that could be taxed.

ISSUE: Is basis based on the fair market value at date of acquisition rather than equity?

HOLDING AND DECISION: (Vinson, C.J.) Yes. Section 113(a)(5) states that the basis for property received by inheritance is the fair market value of the property on the date of acquisition. "Value" is nowhere defined or treated as synonymous with "equity." Therefore, petitioner's basis in the apartment was $262,045, i.e., its fair market value at date of acquisition. The apartment building was an asset subject to exhaustion through wear and tear used in Crane's (P) trade or business. Section 113(b)(1)(B) requires that proper adjustments to basis shall be made in such cases. On sale of the asset, the seller realizes any cash received plus the amount of the indebtedness on the property. This is necessary to compute the selling price which must be subtracted from the taxpayer's adjusted basis to compute a loss or gain on the transaction. Adjusted basis is defined under Section 113(b)(1)(B) as the basis less allowance for depreciation of the asset whether or not actual deductions were taken. The difference between the selling price and Crane's (P) adjusted basis is $23,767.03. Crane (P) actually took most of the deductions allowed her by law. Crane (P) used these deductions to reduce her income. Crane (P) cannot be allowed the benefit of such deduction with no corresponding gain as of the date of sale. Crane (P) actually realized $2,500 in cash plus all her allowable deductions over six years. Affirmed.

EDITOR'S ANALYSIS: In determining profit or loss on the disposition of an asset, liens and other indebtedness are not considered. The formula is fair market value at date of acquisition minus depreciation (if allowed) equals adjusted basis. This is subtracted from the selling price. It is immaterial whether the lien has gotten greater or smaller during the interim. If the selling price is greater than the adjusted basis a profit has been made which is taxable even if, because of an increase in mortgage indebtedness, the taxpayer receives no money.

[For more information on acquisition indebtedness, and the "Crane doctrine," see Casenote Law Outline on Federal Income Taxation, Chapter 4, § I, Basis.]

NOTES:

COMMISSIONER v. TUFTS

461 U.S. 300 (1983).

NATURE OF CASE: Appeal from a deficiency assessment.

FACT SUMMARY: Tufts (P) contended that the assumption of a mortgage which exceeded the fair market value of the property by the purchaser was not a taxable event.

CONCISE RULE OF LAW: The assumption of a non-recourse mortgage constitutes a taxable gain to the mortgagor even if the mortgage exceeds the fair market value of the property.

FACTS: Tufts (P) and others entered into a partnership with Pelt, a builder who had previously entered into an agreement with Farm and Home Savings to transfer a note and deed of trust to the bank in return for a loan to construct an apartment complex in the amount of $1,851,500. The loan was made on a non-recourse basis in that neither the partnership nor the partners assumed personal responsibility for repayment. A year after construction was completed, the partnership could not make the mortgage payments, and each partner sold his interest to Bayles. The fair market value of the property at the time of the transfer did not exceed $1,400,000. As consideration, Bayles paid each partner's sale expenses and assumed the mortgage. The IRS (D) assessed a deficiency against each partner, contending the assumption of the mortgage constituted the creation of taxable gain to each of them which they failed to report. Tufts (P) and the others sued for a redetermination, contending that no gain was realized because the mortgage exceeded the fair market value of the property. The Tax Court upheld the deficiencies, and the court of appeals reversed. The Supreme Court granted certiorari.

ISSUE: Does the assumption of a non-recourse mortgage constitute a taxable gain to the mortgagor even if the mortgage exceeds the fair market value of the property?

HOLDING AND DECISION: (Blackmun, J.) Yes. The assumption of a non-recourse mortgage constitutes a taxable gain to the mortgagor even if the mortgage exceeds the fair market value of the property. When a mortgage is executed, the amount is included, tax free, in the mortgagor's basis of property. The amount is tax free because of the mortgagor's obligation to repay. Unless the outstanding amount of an assumed mortgage is calculated in the seller's amount realized, the money originally received in the mortgage transaction will forever escape taxation. When the obligation to repay is canceled, the mortgagor is relieved of his responsibility to repay the amount he originally received. Therefore he realizes value to the extent of the relief from debt. When the obligation is assumed, it is as if the mortgagor was paid the amount in cash and then paid the mortgage off. As such it is clearly income and taxable. Reversed.

EDITOR'S ANALYSIS: This case illustrates that the cost basis of the property under I.R.C. § 1012 is the cost of the property including any amount paid with borrowed funds. These funds must be included regardless of their source. When property is purchased subject to debt, the purchaser is deemed to have received cash in the amount of the debt, in turn, to have used it to purchase the property.

[For more information on nonrecourse debts, see Casenote Law Outline on Federal Income Taxation, Chapter 4, § II, Amount Realized.]

NOTES:

ESTATE OF FRANKLIN v. COMMISSIONER

544 F.2d 1045 (9th Cir. 1976).

NATURE OF CASE: Appeal from an action seeking disallowance of a taxpayer's deductions.

FACT SUMMARY: Estate of Franklin (P) brought this action against the Tax Commissioner (D) after he sought to disallow deductions for Franklin's and six other doctors' distributive share of losses reported by a limited partnership with respect to its acquisition of a motel.

CONCISE RULE OF LAW: Depreciation is not predicated upon ownership of property but rather upon an investment in property.

FACTS: The Tax Commissioner (D) sought to disallow deductions for the distributive share of losses reported by Twenty-Fourth Property Associates (P), a California limited partnership of seven doctors of which decedent Franklin was one, with respect to its acquisition of a motel and related properties. These losses have their origin in deductions for depreciation and interest claimed with respect to these properties. Under a sales agreement, the owners of the Thunderbird Inn, an Arizona motel, agreed that the property would be paid for over a period of 10 years, with interest on any unpaid balance of 7° percent per annum. Prepaid interest in the amount of $75,000 was payable immediately; monthly principal and interest installments of $9,045 would be paid for approximately the first 10 years, with Associates (P) required to make a balloon payment at the end of the 10 years, forecast as $975,000. The sale was combined with a leaseback of the property by Associates (P) and so they never took physical possession. The Tax Court, agreeing with the Commissioner (D), held that the transaction more nearly resembled an option than a sale, the benefits and burdens of ownership remaining with the original owners. Associates (P) appealed.

ISSUE: Is depreciation predicated upon ownership of property rather than upon an investment in property?

HOLDING AND DECISION: (Sneed, J.) No. An acquisition such as that of Associates (P) if at a price approximately equal to the fair market value of the property under ordinary circumstances would rather quickly yield an equity in the property which the purchaser could not prudently abandon. It meshes with the form of the transaction and constitutes a sale. No such meshing occurs when the purchase price exceeds a demonstrably reasonable estimate of the fair-market value. It is fundamental that depreciation is not predicated upon ownership of property but, rather, upon an investment in property. No such investment exists when payments of the purchase price in accordance with the design of the parties yield no equity to the purchaser. In the transaction before the court, the purchase price payments by Associates (P) have not been shown to constitute an investment in the property. Depreciation was properly disallowed. Only the original owners had an investment in the property. Affirmed.

EDITOR'S ANALYSIS: The court points out that its focus on the relationship of the fair-market value of the property to the unpaid purchase price should not be read as premised upon the belief that a sale is not a sale if the purchaser pays too much. Bad bargains from the buyer's point of view — as well as sensible bargains from buyer's, but exceptionally good from the seller's point of view — do not thereby cease to be sales. See Commissioner v. Brown, 380 U.S. 563 (1965); Union Bank v. United States, 285 F.2d 126 (1961). The holding was limited to transactions substantially similar to the one before the court.

[For more information on acquisition indebtedness, see Casenote Law Outline on Federal Income Taxation, Chapter 4, § I, Basis.]

NOTES:

PLEASANT SUMMIT LAND CORPORATION v. COMMISSIONER

863 F.2d 263 (3rd Cir. 1989), cert. denied, 493 U.S. 901(1989).

NATURE OF CASE: Appeal from disallowance of interest and depreciation deductions.

FACT SUMMARY: After Pleasant & Summit Associates (PSA) (P) acquired the Summit House through the assumption of nonrecourse debt, the limited partners sought to deduct interest charges and depreciation.

CONCISE RULE OF LAW: Interest and depreciation deductions are not allowed for nonrecourse indebtedness that exceeds the fair market value of the property purchased.

FACTS: Prussin (P) was an investor in a limited partnership called PSA (P) which indirectly purchased the Summit House, an apartment building. In the transaction, PSA (P) assumed $2.5 million in deferred nonrecourse debt; a $500,000 cash payment, which may not have been paid; and a $4.7 million mortgage. PSA (P) reported large losses attributable to interest deductions and depreciation and they were passed on to the limited partners, like Prussin (P), who used them to offset income on their individual tax returns. The Commissioner (D) disallowed the entire deductions based on a finding that the nonrecourse debt underlying the purchase of the Summit House was greater than the fair market value of the property. Prussin (P) and PSA (P) appealed.

ISSUE: Are interest and depreciation deductions allowed for nonrecourse indebtedness that exceeds the fair market value of the property purchased?

HOLDING AND DECISION: (Greenberg, J.) No. Interest and depreciation deductions are not allowed for nonrecourse indebtedness that exceeds the fair market value of the property purchased. The Tax Court's factual findings with regard to the fair market value of the Summit House should be upheld since Prussin (P) did not present any expert testimony on value. Accordingly, the only issue left to be decided is the appropriate legal treatment when nonrecourse debt exceeds the fair market value of purchased property. Section 167 of the Internal Revenue Code allows for depreciation deductions based on the cost of property. The cost of property includes the amount of indebtedness incurred or assumed by the purchaser. Section 163 allows for deductions of interest paid for nonrecourse debts. However, prior cases in other circuits have treated the sections identically and determined that these deductions are not available for nonrecourse debt in excess of fair market value. It seems most appropriate to disregard only the portion of the nonrecourse debt in excess of fair market value for purposes of calculating interest and depreciation deductions. Thus, this case is remanded to determine the fair market value of the Summit House and whether PSA (P) made any actual cash investment. PSA (P) and Prussin (P) are entitled to deduct for nonrecourse debt up to the fair market value.

EDITOR'S ANALYSIS: The financing arrangements seen in this case were made solely for the purpose of sheltering income from taxes. The partners of PSA (P) never planned on paying the principal of the debt and would lose nothing since they had no real equity in the property. A different result was reached in the Second Circuit case of Lebowitz v. Commissioner, 917 F.2d 1314 (1990). In that case, the court decided that if the fair market value substantially exceeded the nonrecourse indebtedness, no deductions would be allowed.

[For more information on nonrecourse debt, see Casenote Law Outline on Federal Income Taxation, Chapter 4, § I, Basis.]

NOTES:

AIZAWA v. COMMISSIONER

99 T.C. 197 (1992).

NATURE OF CASE: Appeal from notice of deficiency.

FACT SUMMARY: Aizawa (P) claimed that the amount realized from a foreclosure sale should be the unpaid mortgage principal less the deficiency judgment.

CONCISE RULE OF LAW: The "amount realized" on a foreclosure sale under § 1001 of the Internal Revenue Code is represented by the proceeds of the sale.

FACTS: Aizawa (P) purchased rental property in 1981 for $120,000 and gave the sellers a $90,000 recourse mortgage note with interest only payable until the entire principal was due in June 1985. Aizawa (P) stopped making interest payments in February 1985 and made no payment on the principal. In 1987, the sellers obtained a deficiency judgment of $133,506 in a foreclosure action, which was subsequently reduced to $60,806 after the property was sold for $72,700. Aizawa (P) claimed that this deficiency judgment should be deducted from the unpaid mortgage principal and that the difference ($29,193) was the amount realized for calculating his loss from the original basis of the property. The Commissioner (D) maintained that the $90,000 unpaid mortgage principal constituted the amount realized on the foreclosure sale resulting in a much smaller loss for Aizawa (P).

ISSUE: Is the "amount realized" on a foreclosure sale under § 1001 represented by the proceeds of the sale?

HOLDING AND DECISION: (Tannenwald, J.) Yes. The "amount realized" on a foreclosure sale under § 1001 is represented by the proceeds of the sale. The position of Aizawa (P) in this matter is clearly wrong since it calculates the amount realized by offsetting against the unpaid principal the total amount of the deficiency judgment. However, this deficiency judgment includes not only the unpaid balance but also amounts representing accrued interest, attorneys fees, and court costs. Aizawa (P) has not paid these costs. Still, the Commissioner's (D) position would require Aizawa (P) to treat as money received an amount of his unpaid mortgage principal obligation that has not yet been discharged. If Aizawa (P) is later relieved of the obligation the usual rules of income from discharge will be difficult to apply. Where the discharge of recourse liability is separated from the foreclosure, as in this case, the amount of the proceeds from the sale becomes significant. Thus, the true amount realized under § 1001(a) is simply $72,700 in this case, that is, the amount the property sold for, which can be deducted from Aizawa's (P) original basis to determine his loss. It must be understood that this approach allows Aizawa (P) to deduct a loss that represents borrowed funds which he might not repay and on which he has not yet paid a tax, but the basic rules of cash-basis accounting mandate this result. Therefore, Aizawa's (P) loss is $27,391, representing the difference between his original basis ($100,091) and the $72,700 received in foreclosure.

EDITOR'S ANALYSIS: The court also noted its conclusion was supported by the fact that the result would have been the same under a different scenario. If Aizawa (P) had had the opportunity to sell the property to a third party for $72,700 and the sellers had released the mortgage, the tax consequences would have been the same. In both situations, the mortgage disappears as security and Aizawa's (P) personal obligation to pay the balance of his recourse obligation survives.

[For more information on nonrecourse debt, see Casenote Law Outline on Federal Income Taxation, Chapter 4, § I, Basis.]

NOTES:

Notes

CHAPTER 38
LIKE KIND EXCHANGES

QUICK REFERENCE RULES OF LAW

1. **Multiple Asset Exchanges.** Taxpayers satisfy the holding requirement for like kind exchanges by a lack of intent to liquidate the investment or to use it for personal pursuits. (Bolker v. Commissioner)

   [For more information on like kind exchanges, see Casenote Law Outline on Federal Income Taxation, Chapter 4, § IV, Recognition of Gains and Losses.]

2. **Multiple Asset Exchanges.** Independent sales of old equipment and the purchase of new equipment do not give rise to a like kind exchange. (Bell Lines, Inc. v. United States)

   [For more information on legal title to the property, see Casenote Law Outline on Federal Income Taxation, Chapter 4, § IV, Recognition of Gains and Losses.]

Notes

BOLKER v. COMMISSIONER

760 F.2d 1039 (9th Cir. 1985).

NATURE OF CASE: Appeal from notice of deficiency for invalid like kind exchange.

FACT SUMMARY: Bolker (P), through his corporation, exchanged his property for other property.

CONCISE RULE OF LAW: Taxpayers satisfy the holding requirement for like kind exchanges by a lack of intent to liquidate the investment or to use it for personal pursuits.

FACTS: Bolker (P) was the sole shareholder of Crosby Corporation, the owner of the Montebello property. When Bolker (P) was unable to develop the property himself, he decided to liquidate Crosby and to exchange the Montebello property for other like kind investment property owned by Southern California Savings & Loan (SCS). On the same day, Crosby transferred all of its assets, including the deed to Montebello, and liabilities to Bolker (P) in redemption for the stock. Bolker (P) then contracted with SCS to convey Montebello for certain designated properties. Bolker (P) reported no gain on the transaction, asserting that it qualified for nonrecognition treatment under I.R.C. § 1031(a). The Commmissioner (D) maintained that Bolker (P) did not hold Montebello for productive use in trade or for investment and could not qualify under § 1031. The Tax Court agreed with Bolker (P), and the Commissioner (D) appealed.

ISSUE: Do taxpayers satisfy the holding requirement for like kind exchanges by a lack of intent to liquidate the investment or to use it for personal pursuits?

HOLDING AND DECISION: (Boochever, J.) Yes. Taxpayers satisfy the holding requirement for like kind exchanges by a lack of intent to liquidate the investment or to use it for personal pursuits. Section 1031(a) of the Internal Revenue Code allows for the nonrecognition of property exchange transactions. Nonrecognition is allowed where the taxpayer holds the property for use in business or investment. The continuity of investment is the principle underlying § 1031(a). There appears to be no controlling precedent on this precise issue so the plain language of the statute must govern. Given the ordinary meaning of § 1031, taxpayers satisfy the holding requirement by owning the property and by their lack of intent to liquidate the investment or to use it for personal pursuits. These two requirements are also essentially those placed on the property acquired in a § 1031(a) exchange. Bolker (P) acquired the Montebello property with the intent to exchange it for like-kind property. Therefore, he held Montebello for investment under § 1031(a) and is entitled to nonrecognition. Affirmed.

EDITOR'S ANALYSIS: The Commissioner (D) had cited two revenue rulings in support of his position. The court noted, however, that revenue rulings are not controlling. Furthermore, the court pointed out that the revenue rulings were distinguishable since they did not deal with taxpayers who actually owned and held the property, as did Bolker (P).

[For more information on like kind exchanges, see Casenote Law Outline on Federal Income Taxation, Chapter 4, § IV, Recognition of Gains and Losses.]

NOTES:

BELL LINES v. UNITED STATES
480 F.2d 710 (4th Cir. 1973).

NATURE OF CASE: Appeal from refund of taxes paid.

FACT SUMMARY: Bell Lines (P) sold their old trucks, purchased new trucks, and then claimed depreciation at the full purchase price of the new trucks.

CONCISE RULE OF LAW: Independent sales of old equipment and the purchase of new equipment do not give rise to a like kind exchange.

FACTS: Bell Lines (P) operated an interstate trucking line. In 1959, Bell (P) decided to replace its trucks. Mack submitted the most competitive bid and Bell (P) decided to purchase 148 new trucks. Bell (P) then sold its old trucks to Horner. Unknown to Bell (P), Horner agreed to buy the trucks pursuant to an agreement with Mack whereby Horner could try to make a profit on resale but Mack guaranteed no losses. Ultimately, Mack ended up with title to most of the old trucks and treated the transactions as a trade-in. However, Bell (P) treated the transactions as a purchase and sale and paid capital gains tax on the old trucks and depreciated the new trucks from their full purchase price. The Commissioner (D) maintained that the transactions were a nontaxable exchange of trucks with a downward adjusted basis for the new trucks. The Tax Court ruled for Bell (P), and the Commissioner (D) appealed.

ISSUE: Do independent sales of old equipment and the purchase of new equipment give rise to a like kind exchange?

HOLDING AND DECISION: (Craven, J.) No. Independent sales of old equipment and the purchase of new equipment do not give rise to a like kind exchange. Section 1031(a) of the Internal Revenue Code provides for nonrecognition of like kind exchanges of property. The purpose of this provision is to defer recognition of gain or loss when there is a direct exchange of property. A sale for cash does not qualify even if the money is immediately reinvested in like property. The distinction between an exchange and two separate transactions depends on whether they are mutually dependent transactions. In the present case, Bell's (P) agreement to buy the new trucks was a legal obligation without regard to Horner's purchase of the old trucks. Additionally, there is no evidence that Bell (P) had any knowledge of the Mack-Horner agreement or would not have bought the new trucks without selling the old trucks to Horner. Accordingly, the transactions were independent and do not give rise to the application of § 1031(a). Affirmed.

EDITOR'S ANALYSIS: The court distinguised the Fifth Circuit's decision in Redwing Carriers, Inc. v. Tomlinson, 399 F.2d 652 (1968). In that case, the taxpayer would not have purchased new equipment without a concurrent and binding agreement to sell its old equipment. Revenue ruling 90-34 shows how a transfer may qualify for nonrecognition even where the transferee never holds.

[For more information on legal title to the property, see Casenote Law Outline on Federal Income Taxation, Chapter 4, § IV, Recognition of Gains and Losses.]

NOTES:

CHAPTER 39
INVOLUNTARY CONVERSIONS

QUICK REFERENCE RULES OF LAW

1. **Holding Period of Replacement Property.** In determining whether replacement property acquired by an investor is similar in use to involuntarily converted property, a comparison of the service or use that the properties have to the taxpayer-owner is critical. (Liant Record, Inc. v. Commissioner)

[For more information on involuntary conversions, see Casenote Law Outline on Federal Income Taxation, Chapter 4, § IV, Recognition of Gains and Losses.]

Notes

LIANT RECORD, INC. v. COMMISSIONER

303 F.2d 326 (2nd Cir. 1962).

NATURE OF CASE: Appeal from notice of deficiency for alleged unreported capital gains.

FACT SUMMARY: Liant (P) took the proceeds from a forced sale of a commercial building and acquired three residential apartment buildings.

CONCISE RULE OF LAW: In determining whether replacement property acquired by an investor is similar in use to involuntarily converted property, a comparison of the service or use that the properties have to the taxpayer-owner is critical.

FACTS: Liant (P) owned a twenty-five-story building in Manhattan, New York. The building was leased to eighty-two commerical tenants. In 1953, New York City forced the sale of the building pursuant to condemnation proceedings. Liant (P) received payments for the building in 1954 and 1955 and acquired three pieces of real estate, each containing residential apartment buildings. Liant (P) contended that the gain on the involuntary conversion of the original building was nontaxable under I.R.C. § 1033. The Commissioner (D) maintained that the new apartments were not similar or related in service or use to the condemned office building and asserted that capital gains should have been reported. The Tax Court upheld the Commissioner's (D) deficiency on the ground that the actual physical end use of the offices differed from the end use of the apartments, and Liant (P) appealed.

ISSUE: Is a comparison of the service or use that the properties have to the taxpayer-owner critical in determining whether replacement property acquired by an investor is similar in use to involuntarily converted property?

HOLDING AND DECISION: (Lumbard, J.) Yes. In determining whether replacement property acquired by an investor is similar in use to involuntarily converted property, a comparison of the service or use that the properties have to the taxpayer-owner is critical. Section 1033 of the Internal Revenue Code provides that gains from involuntary conversions of property may be postponed if the taxpayer immediately spends the money in replacing the property. The replacement property must be similar or related in service or use to the converted property. Section 1033 does not allow the taxpayer an opportunity to alter the nature of the investment tax-free. The Tax Court in this case applied a literal "functional test" whereby the physical end use of the properties by the tenants was examined. However, if the taxpayer-owner is an investor rather than a user, it is not the tenant's use but the nature of the lessor's relation to the property which is properly at issue. In the present case, Liant (P) was invested as the owner-lessor of real estate. The Tax Court should have examined the extent and type of Liant's (P) management activity, the amount and kind of services rendered by him to the tenants, and the nature of his business risks connected with the properties. Reversed and remanded.

EDITOR'S ANALYSIS: The standard of § 1033 is similar to that of § 1031 and like kind principles. In 1958, Congress decided that § 1033 was being interpreted too narrowly and amended it to provide for the broader like kind standard. The IRS in Revenue Ruling 64-237 adopted the position of the Liant Record decision, above, by rejecting the functional-use test in favor of the service-or-use-relationship test.

[For more information on involuntary conversions, see Casenote Law Outline on Federal Income Taxation, Chapter 4, § IV, Recognition of Gains and Losses.]

NOTES:

Notes

CHAPTER 40
SALE OF A PRINCIPAL RESIDENCE

QUICK REFERENCE RULES OF LAW

1. **Relationship between Sections 1034 and 121.** A taxpayer is not required to occupy a putative old residence at the time of sale in order to avoid recognition of gain when reinvesting the proceeds in a new principal residence. (Barry v. Commissioner)

   [For more information on recognition of gains, see Casenote Law Outline on Federal Income Taxation, Chapter 4, § IV, Recognition of Gains and Losses.]

2. **Relationship between Sections 1034 and 121.** Taxpayers may qualify for both nonrecognition of gain for sale of a former residence as well as business expense deductions for renting the home prior to sale. (Bolaris v. Commissioner)

   [For more information on recognition of gains, see Casenote Law Outline on Federal Income Taxation, Chapter 4, § IV, Recognition of Gains and Losses.]

Notes

BARRY v. COMMISSIONER

T.C. Memo 1971-179.

NATURE OF CASE: Appeal from notice of deficiency for alleged misapplication of § 1034.

FACT SUMMARY: Barry (P), an Army officer, claimed nonrecognition of gain from the sale of his old house although he had been renting it out while he was stationed overseas.

CONCISE RULE OF LAW: A taxpayer is not required to occupy a putative old residence at the time of sale in order to avoid recognition of gain when reinvesting the proceeds in a new principal residence.

FACTS: Barry (P), a career Army officer, purchased a home in Annapolis for $21,500 in 1955. Barry (P) lived in the home for five years and intended to reside there after his retirement from active duty. However, Barry (P) was ordered to Germany in 1960 and then to Denver in 1962 and lived in government quarters during this period. While he was gone, Barry (P) leased his Annapolis home. In 1965, Barry (P) decided to take a position at the University of Denver Law School after retiring from the Army. Barry (P) then sold his Annapolis home for $30,750 and bought a house in Colorado for $125,000. Barry (P) did not include the gain from the sale of the Annapolis house, claiming nonrecognition under § 1034(a). The Commissioner (D) issued a notice of deficiency, and Barry (P) brought the case to the Tax Court.

ISSUE: Is a taxpayer required to occupy a putative old residence at the time of sale in order to avoid recognition of gain when reinvesting the proceeds in a new principal residence?

HOLDING AND DECISION: (Fay, J.) No. A taxpayer is not required to occupy a putative old residence at the time of sale in order to avoid recognition of gain when reinvesting the proceeds in a new principal residence. Under § 1034, the taxpayer does not recognize gain from the sale of property used as his principal residence if he reinvests the proceeds in a new principal residence. Whether property is considered a principal residence depends upon all the facts and circumstances of an individual case. Property that is held for the production of income does not qualify. In the present case, it is not determinative that Barry (P) rented his Annapolis home and claimed deductions for this property while he was on active duty. Barry (P) did not receive any significant income from the rental and the home was not offered for sale at any time prior to his decision to buy a new home in Colorado. The record shows that Barry (P) always considered the Annapolis house his residence and intended to occupy the home after retirement. Therefore, Barry (P) was entitled to use § 1034 for the nonrecognition of the gain.

EDITOR'S ANALYSIS: The court also noted that Barry (P) was living in government-provided housing during the five years he was away from Maryland under military orders. Thus, he was not able to establish another principal residence. Section 1.1034-1, Income Tax Reg., provides the facts and circumstances which should be examined in making these determinations.

[For more information on recognition of gains, see Casenote Law Outline on Federal Income Taxation, Chapter 4, § IV, Recognition of Gains and Losses.]

NOTES:

BOLARIS v. COMMISSIONER

776 F.2d 1428 (9th Cir. 1985).

NATURE OF CASE: Appeal from disallowance of depreciation and rental expenses deductions.

FACT SUMMARY: The Bolarises (P) bought a new home before selling their old house and sought nonrecognition of both gain on the sale and business expense deductions for renting the old home.

CONCISE RULE OF LAW: Taxpayers may qualify for both nonrecognition of gain for sale of a former residence as well as business expense deductions for renting the home prior to sale.

FACTS: The Bolarises (P) bought a home in 1975 for $44,000 and used it as a principal residence until October, 1977, at which time they bought a new home for $107,000. The old home could not be sold from July, 1977, until August, 1978, when it was purchased for $70,000. During this time, the Bolarises (P) rented the house on a month-to-month basis at fair market value. On the Bolarises' (P) tax return, deductions for depreciation and rental expenses were taken for the old home. Also, they claimed nonrecognition of the gain on the sale since the proceeds were used to purchase a new primary residence. The Commissioner (D) maintained that the Bolarises (P) could not defer recognition and also claim business expense deductions for renting the old house. The Tax Court allowed nonrecognition but denied the deductions.

ISSUE: May taxpayers qualify for both nonrecognition of gain for sale of a former residence as well as business expense deductions for renting the home prior to sale?

HOLDING AND DECISION: (Hall, J.) Yes. Taxpayers may qualify for both nonrecognition of gain for sale of a former residence as well as business expense deductions for renting the home prior to sale. It is well established under § 1034 that the mere fact that a taxpayer temporarily rents out the old house does not prevent deferred recognition of the gain on the sale. Therefore, the Tax Court is affirmed with regard to the application of § 1034. Sections 167(a)(2) and 212 permit depreciation, insurance, and maintenance expense deductions for expenditures on property held for the production of income. The legislative history of § 1034 shows that a former residence can qualify for nonrecognition and also as being held for the production of income. Not all rentals of former residences will qualify for rental expense deductions, especially rentals for less than fair market value. Any windfall that exists is limited to the two-year rollover provision of § 1034. In the present case, the Bolarises (P) rented their old home at fair market value. The old home was permanently abandoned as a residence and offered the Bolarises (P) no elements of personal recreation. Thus, it is apparent that the Bolarises (P) possessed the requisite profit motive when renting their old home. The fact that the rental payments were less than the mortgage payment is not a determinative factor. Therefore, the Bolarises (P) were entitled to the business expense deductions. The Tax Court is reversed on this issue.

CONCURRENCE AND DISSENT: (Reinhardt, J.) Owning a home as a principal residence and owning property for the production of income are mutually exclusive. Prior decisions have long held that business expense deductions are not allowable for expenses incurred with respect to a taxpayer's residence.

EDITOR'S ANALYSIS: The dissent is very persuasive and correctly points out that the plain language of § 1034 seemingly states that property cannot be held for the production of income and also be a principal residence. Further, the dissent points out that the Bolarises (P) would still be entitled to deduct mortgage interest and real taxes paid on the old property.

[For more information on recognition of gains, see Casenote Law Outline on Federal Income Taxation, Chapter 4, § IV, Recognition of Gains and Losses.]

NOTES:

CHAPTER 41
INSTALLMENT SALES

QUICK REFERENCE RULES OF LAW

1. **Installment Sales.** Where a cash-equivalent instrument having a readily ascertainable fair market value is given in exchange for a transfer of property, the value of the instrument must be included in the computation of gain from the transaction. (Warren Jones Company v. Commissioner)

   [For more information on the installment method, see Casenote Law Outline on Federal Income Taxation, Chapter 8, § II, Tax Accounting Methods.]

2. **Installment Sales.** Where the compensation received for a sale is partly or totally indeterminate and speculative, it is an open transaction whereby the seller has no tax assessed on same until his basis in the property sold is recovered. (Burnet v. Logan)

   [For more information on contingent-payment sales, see Casenote Law Outline on Federal Income Taxation, Chapter 4, § IV, Recognition of Gains and Losses.]

Notes

WARREN JONES CO. v. COMMISSIONER

524 F.2d 788 (9th Cir. 1975).

NATURE OF CASE: Appeal from a deficiency tax assessment.

FACT SUMMARY: Warren Jones Co. (P) sold real property receiving $20,000 in cash and an 8%, 15 year mortgage for $133,000.

CONCISE RULE OF LAW: Where a cash-equivalent instrument having a readily ascertainable fair market value is given in exchange for a transfer of property, the value of the instrument must be included in the computation of gain from the transaction.

FACTS: Warren Jones Co. (P) sold real property. Jones (P) received $20,000 plus an 8%, 15 year mortgage for $133,000. Jones (P) claimed no profit from the transaction, the funds actually received being a return of basis. In the alternative, Jones (P) elected to handle the transaction on the installment basis under § 453. That section provides that where the taxpayer receives less than 30% of the sales proceeds in the first year of sale, he may elect to pay taxes on an installment basis as received. The Commissioner denied both contentions and assessed a tax on the difference between Jones' (P) basis and the cash received plus the fair market value of the mortgage which could be discounted to a lender for $118,000. Jones (P) brought suit challenging the Commissioner's (D) contention. The Court found that the mortgage was a liquid asset having a fair market value of $118,000. It further found that Jones would have to place $40,000 in escrow under normal trade practice to guarantee payment of the first $40,000 of the mortgage. Jones' (P) actual realization therefore was $78,000. By subtracting its basis, the taxpayer had realized a substantial capital gain under § 1001. The court found that while the mortgage was a cash-equivalent under § 1001 which would require recognition of the entire gain in the year of sale, because it could not be sold without taking a large loss (42%), the taxpayer could qualify for installment-payment treatment.

ISSUE: If an instrument given in exchange for a transfer of property can readily be sold for an ascertainable amount, may a taxpayer compute gain on the installment method?

HOLDING AND DECISION: (Ely, J.) No. Section 1001 requires that all gain must be reported in the year of transfer when a cash equivalent is given in exchange. Since the mortgage has a fair market value and is readily saleable, it is a cash equivalent within the meaning of the section. The fact that a taxpayer would suffer a substantial loss by selling, or chooses not to do so has no bearing on his tax liability. Once it is found that the exchange involves a cash equivalent, the transaction is deemed complete and gain/loss must be reported for the year of transfer. The Commissioner's (D) determination that the mortgage was a cash equivalent was correct; its value plus the cash received less basis is the measure of Jones' (P) profits, and taxes on this amount must be paid. Reversed.

EDITOR'S ANALYSIS: If an instrument has no fair market value because it is impossible to compute its worth or, because of the risk associated with the transaction, there is no market, the installment method may be utilized, e.g. Burnet v Logan, 283 U.S. 404. For example, in In re Steen, 509 F.2d 1398 (9th Cir. 1975), payment of the instrument depended on a favorable decision of a suit involving a novel question of state law. There was no way that a fair market value could be determined, and no one would purchase the note.

[For more information on the installment method, see Casenote Law Outline on Federal Income Taxation, Chapter 8, § II, Tax Accounting Methods.]

NOTES:

BURNET v. LOGAN

283 U.S. 404 (1931).

NATURE OF CASE: Commissioner's (D) appeal from a Tax Court reversal of his decision to assess deficiencies on a closed sale.

FACT SUMMARY: When Youngstown Sheet and Pipe purchased their shares in Andrews and Hitchcock Co., Logan (P) and the other shareholders received, among other things, 60 cents per ton of ore mined each year from a particular leased mine. The Commissioner (D) found this was an ascertainable value and called it a closed transaction, making payments subject to allocation between return of capital and income.

CONCISE RULE OF LAW: Where the compensation received for a sale is partly or totally indeterminate and speculative, it is an open transaction whereby the seller has no tax assessed on same until his basis in the property sold is recovered.

FACTS: The shareholders of Andrews and Hitchcock Iron, including Logan (P), sold their shares to Youngstown Sheet and Pipe for a sum less than fair market value and an agreement to pay them 60 cents per ton for ore mined each year under a 97-year lease covering a specific mine. The lease did not require any minimum or maximum amount of ore to be mined each year. Logan (P) owned 250 of the 4,000 shares in Andrews and Hitchcock, for which she received the aforementioned compensation. She also was paid one-half of the payments accruing to her mother's estate, as such was the mandate of the will. This was valued for estate purposes at $277,000. Because she had not yet recovered her basis in her own stock or the assessed value on her mother's stock, Logan (P) did not pay taxes on the amounts she received. The Commissioner (D) held that the iron ore payments to be made by Youngstown had an ascertainable value, the sale constituted a closed transaction, and each payment must be allocated between income and a return of capital. The court of appeals overruled the district court's affirmation of the Commissioner's (D) position and allowed Logan (P) to escape assessments until she recovered her basis, holding the transaction was an open one. This appeal by the Commissioner (D) followed.

ISSUE: If the compensation to be received for sale of property is indeterminate and speculative, is the seller entitled to recover his basis before any tax can be assessed on the transaction?

HOLDING AND DECISION: (McReynolds, J.) Yes. Where the value of the compensation cannot be determined, as in this case, there exists an open transaction which requires a return of basis before any taxes can be assessed thereon. It is obvious that nobody can ascertain what 60 cents per ton will be worth or is worth when there is no minimum or maximum amount to be mined under the lease, Youngstown's future needs are unpredictable, and the value of the ore left in the mine is uncertain. Thus, in this open transaction, the compensation payments are not subject to tax until if and when Logan (P) recovers her basis therein. Thereafter, any payments constitute gain and are taxable as such. This basis, insofar as Logan's (P) inheritance from her mother's estate, is equal to her mother's basis. Taking all of this into account, we must overrule the Commissioner (D) and affirm the decision of the court of appeal.

EDITOR'S ANALYSIS: Had there been a method to estimate the value of the ore payment, the court would probably have accepted it readily. It is, after all, a predisposition on the part of the courts to value property whenever possible to provide a basis, even a rough one. This arises from the desire to subject all property to tax when it is first proper to do so, avoiding deferral of revenue collection beyond the necessary time.

[For more information on contingent-payment sales, see Casenote Law Outline on Federal Income Taxation, Chapter 4, § IV, Recognition of Gains and Losses.]

NOTES:

CHAPTER 42
SALE OF A BUSINESS AND SALE-LEASEBACKS

QUICK REFERENCE RULES OF LAW

1. **Sale-Leaseback Characterized as Tax-Free Exchange.** The assets of a business must be separately treated to determine if income from their sales is capital or ordinary based on § 1221. (Williams v. McGowan)

   [For more information on definition of capital gains and losses, see Casenote Law Outline on Federal Income Taxation, Chapter 4, § V, Capital Gains and Losses.]

2. **Sale-Leaseback Characterized as Tax-Free Exchange.** The intent of the parties at the time of the dissolution determines whether a portion of the buyout price was allocated for a covenant not to compete. (Annabelle Candy Co. v. Commissioner)

3. **Sale-Leaseback Characterized as Tax-Free Exchange.** Where there is a genuine multiple-party transaction with economic substance which is compelled or encouraged by business or regulatory realities is imbued with tax independent considerations and is not shaped solely by tax avoidance features which have meaningless labels attached the form of the transaction adopted by the parties should govern for tax purposes. (Frank Lyon Co. v. United States)

   [For more information on property transfer transactions see Casenote Law Outline on Federal Income Taxation Chapter 5, § V Characterization Issues.]

4. **Sale-Leaseback Characterized as Tax-Free Exchange.** Where property is sold for its approximate fair market value, the presence of a long term leaseback will not render the sale an exchange. (Leslie Co. v. Commissioner)

   [For more information on gain or loss on exchange of property, see Casenote Law Outline on Federal Income Taxation, Chapter 4, § IV, Recognition of Gains and Losses.]

Notes

WILLIAMS v. McGOWAN

152 F.2d 570 (2nd Cir. 1945).

NATURE OF CASE: Appeal by Commissioner.

FACT SUMMARY: Williams (P) sold his going business after buying out his deceased partner's interest in it.

CONCISE RULE OF LAW: The assets of a business must be separately treated to determine if income from their sales is capital or ordinary based on § 1221.

FACTS: Williams (P) and Reynolds formed a partnership. When Reynolds died, Williams (P) purchased Reynolds' interest from the estate. Williams (P) then sold the assets of the business to a third party. Williams (P) reported the sale as an ordinary loss on his tax return. The Commissioner (D) determined that the business was a capital asset which demanded capital gains treatment.

ISSUE: Does the sale of a sole proprietorship result in capital gains and losses?

HOLDING AND DECISION: (Learned Hand, J.) No. While it has been held that a partner's interest in a going concern should he treated as a capital asset, when Williams (P) bought Reynolds' share, the business became a sole proprietorship. There is no suggestion of a tax avoidance scheme, and the business must be treated as a sole proprietorship. Since there is no special treatment designated for a sole proprietorship, we must examine § 1221 in order to determine the appropriate tax treatment. Section 1221 requires that all assets be treated as capital ones unless they fit within three exceptions, i.e. stock in trade, property held primarily for resale to customers, and depreciable business property. Williams (P) transferred cash, receivables, fixtures, and inventory. Fixtures are depreciable, and inventory is primarily held for customer resale. Therefore neither of these assets is subject to capital gains treatment. Cash transfers cannot result in gains or losses. Therefore, the only asset which might be deemed capital in nature is the receivables. However, it had not been argued whether they are subject to depreciation. Therefore, the case is remanded to the district court for a decision on this point. All other assets should be treated as yielding ordinary income.

DISSENT: (Frank, J.) The parties, in their contract, stated that Williams (P) was to transfer his "rights, title and interest . . . in, and to, the hardware business." I believe that Congress did not intend to carve the sale of a business into separate distinct sales. The parties transacted for the sale and purchase of the business as a whole. There does not seem to be any rationale to support the majority's decision either on a contract theory or on the purpose of § 1221 as I perceive it. What was sold was the business, not the individual assets. For this reason, I dissent.

EDITOR'S ANALYSIS: Goodwill is considered a capital asset when a business is sold. Rev. Rul. 57-480, 1957-2 C.B. 47; Regs. § 1.167(a)-3. On the other hand, accounts receivable acquired on the sale of inventory property will be deemed non-capital assets, § 1221(4). Since most businesses are on the accrual basis, the receivables will already have been reported as income so that § 1221(4) will have little effect on them. It may be more significant for cash basis taxpayers.

[For more information on definition of capital gains and losses, see Casenote Law Outline on Federal Income Taxation, Chapter 4, § V, Capital Gains and Losses.]

NOTES:

ANNABELLE CANDY CO. v. COMMISSIONER

314 F.2d 1 (9th Cir. 1962).

NATURE OF CASE: Appeal from notice of deficiency.

FACT SUMMARY: Sommers (P) left the Annabelle Candy partnership and claimed that a portion of the buyout price was for a covenant not to compete.

CONCISE RULE OF LAW: The intent of the parties at the time of the dissolution determines whether a portion of the buyout price was allocated for a covenant not to compete.

FACTS: Altshuler and Sommers (P) were equal partners in Annabelle Candy (P). They had a distinctive method of making Rocky Road candy. When differences between the partners surfaced, a negotiated buyout of Sommers (P) was arranged. The agreement provided for a total consideration of $115,000 to be paid to him in installments. Sommers (P) also agreed not to compete or engage in any activities that might be prejudicial to the business for a period of five years. These restrictive covenants were discussed after the price was agreed upon, but were a critical part of the contract. On his tax return, Sommers (P) allocated $80,000 of the total purchase price to the covenant not to compete and began amortization of the allocated portion over the five years of the covenant. The Commissioner (D) disallowed this deduction maintaining that the entire buyout price was for his share of the business rather than for a restrictive covenant. The Tax Court sustained the Commissioner's (D) deficiency notice, and Sommers (P) appealed.

ISSUE: Does the intent of the parties at the time of the dissolution determine whether a portion of the buyout price was allocated for a covenant not to compete?

HOLDING AND DECISION: (Barnes, J.) Yes. The intent of the parties at the time of the dissolution determines whether a portion of the buyout price was allocated for a covenant not to compete. Section 167(a)(1) authorizes taxpayers to use a depreciation deduction for property used in trade or business. There is no question that a covenant not to compete for a definite term qualifies under this section. However, in order to amortize a payment for a restrictive covenant there must be an actual payment for the covenant. To determine whether the covenant has been paid for, the terms of the contract should be examined. Additionally, it is proper to look behind the contract to the intentions of the parties. In the present case, the buyout agreement does not contain any allocation of consideration for the covenant. However, the Tax Court did not strictly determine whether there was an intention, at the time the parties signed the agreement, to allocate a portion of the price to the covenant. Therefore, the case must be remanded for this determination.

EDITOR'S ANALYSIS: The court also noted that Sommers (P) would have the burden of proving that a portion of the buyout price was allocated to a covenant not to compete. It appears from the decision that there were negative tax consequences to Altshuler, the other partner, from allocating part of the price to the covenant. Sommers (P) will have an extremely difficult case to show that the parties intended to allocate given the fact that it appeared that he unilaterally decided an amount of allocation after the fact.

NOTES:

FRANK LYON CO. v. UNITED STATES

435 U.S. 561 (1978).

NATURE OF CASE: Appeal from denial of a tax refund.

FACT SUMMARY: A bank entered into a sale-leaseback arrangement with Frank Lyon Co. (P).

CONCISE RULE OF LAW: Where there is a genuine multiple-party transaction with economic substance which is compelled or encouraged by business or regulatory realities is imbued with tax independent considerations and is not shaped solely by tax avoidance features which have meaningless labels attached the form of the transaction adopted by the parties should govern for tax purposes.

FACTS: When the Federal Reserve System nixed Worthen Bank's plan to finance its own building Worthen sought other financing and wound up with a sale-and-leaseback arrangement by which Frank Lyon Co. (P) whose principal stockholder was a bank director would buy the building as Worthen put it up and lease it back to Worthen. The primary lease term was 25 years with options to extend for 40 more years. Lyon (P) was the sole party directly liable on the permanent mortgage loan from an insurance company Worthen was to take care of the expenses usually associated with maintaining a building and the rent was set at just enough to cover interest and principal on the mortgage loan. Noting that Lyon (P) would receive nothing on its investment for 30 years the Commissioner disallowed the depreciation and building-related deductions on the ground that Lyon was not the owner of the building but merely a financing party. Lyon (P) sued for a tax refund and won but there was a reversal on appeal.

ISSUE: If the parties set their transaction for a form with some substance will it govern for tax purposes?

HOLDING AND DECISION: (Blackmun J.) Yes. The form of the transaction adopted by the parties should govern for tax purposes where there is a genuine multiple-party transaction with economic substance which is compelled or encouraged by business or regulatory realities it is imbued with tax independent considerations and it is not shaped solely by tax avoidance features which have meaningless labels attached. In this case the presence of a third-party lender distinguishes this from many two-party sale-leaseback cases where the form was merely a tax avoidance device. Here Lyon (P) was liable on the mortgage loan and exposed its business well-being to a real and substantial risk. The form was not a sham and is to be respected. Reversed.

DISSENT: (Stevens J.) Since Worthen has at present the unrestricted right to control the residual value of the property for a price not exceeding the cost of its unamortized financing it is the owner.

EDITOR'S ANALYSIS: It is clear that the majority was much impressed by the fact that a regulatory agency prohibited Worthen from financing its own building. However this transaction might be viewed as an indirect means for Worthen to do what it could not do directly.

[For more information on property transfer transactions see Casenote Law Outline on Federal Income Taxation Chapter 5 § V Characterization Issues.]

NOTES:

LESLIE CO. v. COMMISSIONER

539 F.2d 943 (3d Cir. 1976).

NATURE OF CASE: Appeal from the denial of a loss deduction.

FACT SUMMARY: In order to obtain financing for a new plant, Leslie (P) had to agree to a sale and leaseback of it to Prudential Ins. Co.

CONCISE RULE OF LAW: Where property is sold for its approximate fair market value, the presence of a long term leaseback will not render the sale an exchange.

FACTS: Leslie Co. (P) wished to construct a new plant. Leslie (P) was unable to obtain financing. Prudential Insurance agreed to advance $2,400,000 for the construction of the plant. After construction, Leslie (P) was to sell Prudential the plant for $2,400,000 or its actual construction cost whichever was less. Leslie then would sign a 30 year lease with two ten year options. The plant cost $3,187,000 to build. Upon completion, Leslie "sold" the building to Prudential for $2,400,000. A loss of $787,000 was reported from the "sale." The Commissioner (D) denied the loss based on the rationale in Century Electric, alleging that this was an exchange. The court found that the fair market value of the property was approximately $2,400,000 and that the transaction was a sale with a concurrent condition requiring a lease. Since the sale was for the full market value of the plant, the lease had no capital value, and Leslie (P) was entitled to deduct the entire amount.

ISSUE: Where property is sold for its approximate fair market value, will the presence of a long term leaseback render the transaction an exchange?

HOLDING AND DECISION: (Garth, J.) No. Where the sale is for the fair market value of the property, the presence of a long term leaseback will not render the transaction an exchange. Regulation 1.1002(d) states that an exchange must involve the reciprocal transfer of property. If the sale is for the fair market value of the asset/property, the lease has no separate value, but is merely a condition of sale. Under this regulation, the transaction cannot be deemed an exchange. We find that valuation of the property is the key to such transactions. Congress did not intend § 1002 to require taxes on paper transactions. However, where there is a transfer of property for cash which is the equivalent of the property's fair market value, the transaction is a sale, and a loss may be taken on it. Affirmed.

EDITOR'S ANALYSIS: The underlying distinction between Century and Leslie is that in Leslie the sale was tax motivated. No valid business purpose was served except acquiring additional cash. The transaction was a mere sham to acquire a friendly landlord, cash, and a deduction. A typical device to avoid the effects of § 1031 is the so-called 3-cornered transaction. Property is first sold and then the proceeds are reinvested in like assets. This is a sale under current tax law interpretations.

[For more information on gain or loss on exchange of property, see Casenote Law Outline on Federal Income Taxation, Chapter 4, § IV, Recognition of Gains and Losses.]

NOTES:

CHAPTER 43
TIME VALUE OF MONEY: ORIGINAL ISSUE DISCOUNT AND RELATED MATTERS

QUICK REFERENCE RULES OF LAW

1. **Interaction of Sections 467 and 1274.** Capital gains treatment applies only to situations in which appreciation in value accrues over a substantial period of time. (United States v. Midland-Ross Corporation)

    [For more information on capital gains, see Casenote Law Outline on Federal Income Taxation, Chapter 4, § V, Capital Gains and Losses.]

Notes

UNITED STATES v. MIDLAND-ROSS CORPORATION

381 U.S. 54 (1965).

NATURE OF CASE: Appeal from deficiency notice for failure to treat gains as ordinary income.

FACT SUMMARY: Midland-Ross (P) sought to treat earned original issue discount as capital gains.

CONCISE RULE OF LAW: Capital gains treatment applies only to situations in which appreciation in value accrues over a substantial period of time.

FACTS: Midland-Ross (P) bought noninterest-bearing promissory notes from the issuers at prices discounted below the face amounts. Midland-Ross (P) held these notes for over six months and then sold them for more than the issue price, but still less than the face amount. Midland-Ross (P) sought capital gains treatment for its profit rather than declaring the gain as ordinary income. The Commissioner (D) issued a notice of deficiency, but Midland-Ross (P) prevailed on its suit for a refund in the district court and court of appeals. The Commissioner (D) petitioned for certiorari, and the Supreme Court granted review.

ISSUE: Does capital gains treatment apply only to situations in which appreciation in value accrues over a substantial period of time?

HOLDING AND DECISION: (Brennan, J.) Yes. Capital gains treatment applies only to situations in which appreciation in value accrues over a substantial period of time. Capital gains treatment applies only to gains on the sale or exchange of a capital asset. However, not everything that is called property in the ordinary sense qualifies as a capital asset. The term "capital asset" must be construed narrowly in accordance with the purpose of Congress to give capital gains treatment only for appreciations in value accrued over a long period of time. Earned original issue discount serves the same function as stated interest; it is the equivalent of compensation for the use of money to the date of sale. Unlike typical capital appreciations, the earning of discount to maturity is predictable and measurable. Therefore, since earned original issue discount is so similar to stated interest income, it must be treated as ordinary income. Thus, Midland-Ross (P) should have reported its gain from the purchase and sale of discounted notes as ordinary income. Reversed.

EDITOR'S ANALYSIS: This decision resolved a conflict between the courts of appeals on this issue. In the instant case, Midland-Ross (P) sold the notes in the same year of purchase. Thus, the Court did not reach the question of whether accrual-basis taxpayers would be required to report discount earned before final disposition of the obligation.

[For more information on capital gains, see Casenote Law Outline on Federal Income Taxation, Chapter 4, § V, Capital Gains and Losses.]

NOTES:

Notes

Notes